Finding the Hot Spots

Finding the Hot Spots
10 Strategies for Global Investing

David Riedel

WILEY

John Wiley & Sons, Inc.

Published by John Wiley & Sons, Inc., Hoboken, New Jersey
Published simultaneously in Canada

For general information on our other products and services or for technical support, please contact our Customer Care Department within the United States at (800) 762-2974, outside the United States at (317) 572-3993 or fax (317) 572-4002.

Wiley also publishes its books in a variety of electronic formats. Some content that appears in print may not be available in electronic books. For more information about Wiley products, visit our web site at www.wiley.com.

Library of Congress Cataloging-in-Publication Data:

Riedel, David, 1967-
    Finding the hot spots : ten strategies for investors / David Riedel.
        p. cm.
    ISBN-13: 978-0-471-77377-1 (cloth)
    ISBN-10: 0-471-77377-8
    1. Investments, Foreign.   2. Investments, American.   3. Stock exchanges.
4. Investment analysis.   I. Title.
    HG4538.R49 2006
    332.6—dc22   2006008034

Printed in the United States of America

10 9 8 7 6 5 4 3 2 1

To my parents for opening my eyes to the world,
To Annie for opening my world and
To Ellie for opening my eyes.

Contents

Chapter ONE

Invest Internationally for Yourself

Investing in anything involves careful consideration of risk and reward. You need to weigh the potential profit against the risk that something will go other than expected and generate losses. Thousands of investors make investment decisions every day. They assess the information that is available, consider their own circumstances, evaluate any new information to gauge whether it changes their view or belief, and decide to buy, sell, or hold a particular investment. If, for example, Apple releases a new version of the iPod, investors have to consider the impact on the company's financial outlook, assess whether the current price of the shares is too high or too low relative to that outlook, and evaluate how a computer/consumer electronics stock fits into their portfolio. Once these factors have been considered, a decision to buy, sell, or hold Apple shares is made.

1

This book argues that the same consideration should be given to shares in international companies. A thoughtful view on the outlook for a particular industry, company, or country might lead you to decide to look for a way to invest in stock of a particular international company. This book is your guide to identifying, buying, and following investments in international companies. Surprisingly few individual investors choose to use the hundreds of international stocks listed on the various exchanges in the United States to diversify their portfolios and profit from the tremendous economic growth worldwide.

This book focuses on investors buying individual stocks in non-U.S. companies. As it explains later, hundreds of non-U.S. companies have stocks that trade in the United States and are as easy for individual investors to buy as stocks from IBM, Coca-Cola, and Disney. Some investors might choose to use mutual funds to invest in international markets, but as you will see, this practice is of dubious value and can be quite expensive.

The world is shrinking—you need to be invested in international markets. If you look around this very minute, no matter where you are, you will see the effect of global trade and development. The computer I am using to write this book was made by a Japanese company and manufactured in China. The screen was produced in Taiwan and the keyboard is from a Korean company. The coffee I am drinking is from Indonesia and the mug was made in Thailand. My shirt was made in Macau, pants in Brazil, and underwear in Hong Kong.

The wine I had with dinner last night was French; the chocolate in the dessert was Belgian. Not that I have anything against things made in the United States—the taxis and subway cars I ride in are American, my house was built by excellent American construction workers, the bank that I use is a U.S. bank, my business cards were printed in New Jersey, and the plane I took on my last trip was made by a U.S. company. Think about it yourself. Take a minute to look around you. Chances are that a good portion of the things in your home, your office, and your life in general are imported or somehow influenced by global trade and the world economy. Your portfolio should be as well.

Conventional wisdom is that 20 percent of your stock holdings should be international. Most U.S. investors have far less than this. In fact, this percentage is a bit outdated, and I contend that, at this point, a third of your holdings should be in non-U.S. companies. Having a third of your holdings in international stocks better reflects the role of international companies, trade, and worldwide development in our everyday lives. Look around again and think about your life—more than a third of the things in your life are imported. Your portfolio should reflect that reality of modern life.

Why do so many individual investors ignore the tremendous opportunities in international equities?   There are a number of misconceptions about investing in international stocks.

Investing in international stocks is too risky.   Fear of

the unknown keeps many people from buying stocks in individual international companies. There is a somewhat justified concern that the risk in international companies is higher than in U.S. companies. However, if the risks are higher, the rewards and potential profits are higher still. When was the last time one of your U.S. stock holdings doubled in a matter of weeks? It has probably been a while. Don't forget: There are risks, but there are risks in investing in U.S. companies as well. Remember Enron and WorldCom? Nobody would ever tell you that you should not buy stocks from a beacon of American business like IBM, Coca-Cola, Disney, Time Warner, Blockbuster, Microsoft, or Sears. Yet in half of these examples a three-year investment would have lost you money. My point is that while there are risks in investing in international stocks, there are also risks in investing in domestic stocks.

I can't invest in international markets; my broker deals only in U.S. stocks. Hogwash. Stocks in hundreds of international companies trade on the New York Stock Exchange (NYSE), American Stock Exchange (AMEX), and NASDAQ. Companies from China, Brazil, Poland, South Africa, and India trade in the United States just as easily as Citibank and General Motors. Details in Chapter 2 will show you just how many great options there are for investing in international companies in the U.S. markets.

How can I possibly understand an international company? Stocks that are listed in the United States are

4

required to disclose information about their financial performance and the status of their business. Just as Google and Home Depot must tell the public about their business performance through quarterly announcements, foreign companies have to provide the SEC with periodic updates on the financial and operational performance of their business. Furthermore, not every person who owns shares in Google, for example, fully understands the details of the company's search technology. What they do understand is that the company earned profits of $592 million on revenue of $2.25 billion in the quarter ended March 31, 2006. You can certainly find out enough information about an international company to make a smart investment decision.

It is too hard to assess the risk in investing in an international company. Given the availability of the same information on international companies listed in the United States as on U.S. companies listed here, this argument does not hold up. A bit of additional digging might be required to fully understand the political and economic situation in the countries in question that might impact the value of investments in these companies, but the Internet makes this much more manageable than it was a few years ago. Through Yahoo!Finance (www.yahoo.com), the Bank of New York ADR site (www.bnyadr.com), and Google searches, a wide variety of sources such as English-language news media, company profiles, industry information, and financial web sites can be found.

Political risk is too high. There is certainly an element of political risk in international investing that does not really exist in investing in the United States—the chance that something will change on the political front in a country where you are invested. That is why you should demand a better return in the international markets. Even within the various international markets, you should demand higher upside potential to make an investment in, say, Thailand versus Great Britain. Political risk is certainly there, but through diversification and adequate assessment of the risk-and-return balance, you should be able to properly account for it in your portfolio.

International companies cannot be trusted to provide reliable information. As you'll learn in Chapter 2, the information that an international company must provide to the public in order to be listed in the United States has to be checked by a reliable auditing firm and the company has to attest to the fact that it is accurate. This is not always foolproof, and there are certainly examples of companies providing unreliable information. Note, however, that this risk is not limited to international companies. Enron and WorldCom are good, albeit obvious, examples of the reality that U.S. companies don't necessarily always provide accurate information.

I would rather just use a mutual fund to invest in international markets. This strategy seems boring, but it can be appropriate for some people. Mutual funds offer the benefit of easy diversification and the fact that you can simply buy them and leave the management of the portfolio to someone else. Keep in mind, however, that over the longer term, something like 90 percent of actively managed funds do not do as well as the underlying index. Furthermore, buying a fund is like being a passenger in somebody else's car—the fund managers make all the decisions, get most of the glory, and have all the fun. Reading a quarterly report from your mutual fund tells you a bit about what is owned in the fund and how it has performed, but this is not nearly as interesting as following individual stocks that you hold in your portfolio yourself and making the decision of when to buy, sell, or hold them. Many people enjoy the challenge and have the time, energy, and inclination to buy individual stocks rather than mutual funds.

Remember that mutual fund companies charge fees for managing your money and tend to be somewhat conservative in their investment approach. The goal of a fund manager is for the fund to perform better than the market as a whole and to prevent big meltdowns in the portfolio. If the S&P 500 Index is up 5 percent in a year, the goal of a fund manager investing in those stocks is to have the value of the portfolio increase at least 7 percent in that same year. The extra 2 percent should cover the fees (the average expense ratio for an actively managed fund is about 1.5 percent) and indicates that investors did better by having that manager manage their money rather than just putting it in an index fund or some alternative that does not have many fees associated with it.

A 2 percent fee might sound low enough to be dismissed as inconsequential, but over a 10-year period, a 2 percent fee on an investment of $10,000 costs the investor nearly $6,000 in fees and forgone earnings. Some people prefer to leave individual stock picking to the professionals, but remember that they usually do not do any better than the underlying index—and it takes the fun out of investing, for those who enjoy it.

I'll just buy stock in large U.S. companies that do business overseas to get international exposure into my portfolio. Many individual investors believe that owning stock in companies like IBM, Disney, and Coca-Cola, which do business overseas, is an adequate way to get exposure to international markets. There are two things wrong with this notion. First, stock in those large multinational corporations tends to perform pretty much in line with the U.S. stock market. Second, though these companies might have some operations overseas, the bulk of their profits likely come from the United States.

Following international stocks is interesting and educational. Staying abreast of international news—especially international business news—is interesting and educational. There is plenty of international news available to anyone interested in reading it. You can't pick up a newspaper without getting some information about what is going on in the world. Reading the international news teaches us about other countries, industries, and people. Having information about the impact of growing wealth among the population of a country like India, China, Indonesia, or Brazil puts those people in some sort of context for us to contemplate and consider. How will the Internet develop in China? Do people in these countries have personal computers and telephone lines? Who is meeting the challenge of getting telephone service to rural parts of India and Pakistan? What is going on in Turkey as it joins the European Union? Chapter 4 discusses how to use the headlines to learn about trends, industries, countries, and investments that you might want to add to your portfolio. As the world shrinks and global developments impact our daily lives, investments can be a way to stay on top of these developments and help us learn more about the world around us—while profiting at the same time!

Chapter TWO

Think Globally, Invest Locally

Investing in a wide range of attractive and interesting foreign companies is as easy as picking up the phone. Your broker or online account is a direct line to all of the investment ideas discussed in this book. You do not have to set up an account in Zimbabwe to buy African mining stocks. Nor do you have to be a resident of Japan to invest in stocks in that market. Many foreign companies have chosen to list in the U.S. markets in order to tap into the largest and most liquid equity market in the world. Some of these are direct listings whereby the company simply trades on the New York Stock Exchange (NYSE), the American Stock Exchange (AMEX), or the NASDAQ. Others are American Depositary Receipts (ADRs), which trade like regular stocks but represent the stocks rather than being stocks themselves. No need to get too confused here—you can buy and sell these

ADRs just like any other stock in your portfolio. We will walk through this process later in the chapter.

Buying Stocks in Foreign Markets

Many countries have regulations that do not allow for-eigners to have brokerage accounts. In addition, many monitor closely, tax, or prevent outright the transfer of funds overseas. Even in places that allow you to have an account, it is not worthwhile for most individuals to go thorough the hassle of setting up a brokerage account in a foreign country to buy and sell stocks there. Certainly there are lots of interesting stocks in Austria, Japan, India, and Australia that you can trade in if you have an account in one of those countries, but there are defi-nitely problems with setting up an account that would let you do it.

You could use the Internet to find a broker who seems reputable, file the forms to open an account, and wire money in to get started, but that is just where the hassles would begin. How do you state any gains or losses on your tax returns? If you want to bring the prof-its back to a U.S. bank, there is a good chance you will attract unwanted attention from the bank authorities, let alone the tax collector. Since the establishment of the Patriot Act, banks are required to be on the lookout for suspicious transfers of money. Wiring more than a few thousand dollars to an account overseas is likely to raise some serious red flags. Trying to take that money out of the foreign country will probably raise issues on both sides—with the money leaving the foreign country and with the funds arriving at your bank. These issues are not insurmountable, but they are an inconvenience that is not necessary, given the large number of international stocks that trade right here in the United States.

Direct Listings

The U.S. equity market is the largest and most liquid equity market in the world. Routinely trading more than $50 billion per day, investors around the world appreciate the ability to trade freely in the market. In addition, investors take comfort in the fact that the Securities and Exchange Commission (SEC) and National Association of Securities Dealers (NASD) are carefully monitoring the market, the companies that are listed on it, and the brokers and dealers who trade in it to ensure that the market is functioning well and smoothly. Restrictions on activities such as insider trading, the sharing of inside information, and taking advantage of other investors in the market are among the strictest in the world. Newspapers frequently offer stories of people accused of trading on information that should not have been shared with them. This market integrity is not as common in many overseas markets and it is one reason that the U.S. market is so attractive to investors. Because the U.S. equity market attracts so many investors, it attracts a lot of companies as well.

Companies choose to go through the regulatory hurdles required to list in the U.S. markets because they know that this accomplishes two very important things for them. First, surviving the regulatory scrutiny to get listed in the United States creates prestige and credibility with customers, suppliers, banks, and others in their home market. If you are the only Turkish textile company listed in the United States, you separate yourself from the others as a more trustworthy supplier, borrower, or customer. Rightly or wrongly, having survived the microscope of the U.S. regulators provides instant credibility. Second, companies list in the United States because investors there are willing to finance businesses, technologies, concepts, and ideas like nowhere else in the world. Though a wide variety of businesses attract investment in markets around the world, the U.S. market, because of its size and liquidity, is the best place to raise money from investors.

In recent years, the trend of listing in the United States has accelerated. Companies ranging from Dutch sports equipment company Head to Brazilian bank Banco Itaú are directly listed on the NYSE in the United States. Other companies are listed on the NASDAQ or on the AMEX.

There is absolutely no difference between buying shares in Microsoft or Wal-Mart and buying shares in Greek shipping company Diana (DSX) or Chinese fertilizer company Bodisen Biotech (BBC). Through your online brokerage account or through your broker, you can buy and sell shares in these foreign companies the same way you do with U.S. companies. They often pay dividends (in U.S. dollars), report their results quarterly, file statements with the SEC when material developments take place, and hold shareholder meetings open to all shareholders, just like U.S. companies.

American Depositary Receipts (ADRs)

Despite their fancy name, American Depositary Receipts are simply a way to invest in a stock. This is not a warrant or option or anything like that; you should look at it as being just the same as a stock. Basically, it is a convenient way for investors to buy and own overseas stocks.

Consider Nokia, for example. Nokia shares do not actually trade in the United States, but you can buy shares in Nokia by buying NOK shares on the NYSE. These ADRs were created by a U.S. bank that bought a big block of Nokia shares in Europe and holds them in custody. The bank then issues receipts (ADRs) on these shares to investors, who effectively own the shares in the custody. This way, everything trades in U.S. dollars, on a U.S. exchange, with all of the settlement and logistics in the United States. Thus, there is no need to convert to a non-U.S. currency, and settlement is faster and smoother. So if you were enthusiastic about the new Nokia phone that you bought and wanted to invest in the company, you could study the company and its prospects, make sure that it fits into your portfolio, and, through your broker or online brokerage account, buy the NOK shares on the NYSE. The value of the receipts would fluctuate along with the price of Nokia shares in Europe.

Many foreign companies have chosen to list ADRs in the United States to benefit from the advantages of the large and liquid equity markets here. Numerous Latin American companies began to list shares in the United States in the 1980s. The first one to attract attention from the mass market was Teléfonos de México, or Telmex, the Mexican telephone company, which listed in the United States in 1991. These shares quickly became popular with individuals and institutions. A foreign company with high growth prospects listed in the United States constitutes a unique opportunity to invest in the growth

Telmex ADRs trade on the New York Stock Exchange under ticker TMX. Like buying shares in Microsoft under ticker MSFT, when you buy shares under the ticker TMX, you will be participating in the fortunes of that company. Right now, if you pay the $20.80 price for one share of TMX, you will be the proud owner of 20 shares of Telmex. The ratio of the number of shares that are represented by each ADR varies by company. In the case of Telmex, it is 1:20 (1 ADR represents 20 individual shares).

and prospects of that company and country—exactly what I am trying to explain in this book.

Over-the-Counter Bulletin Board Stocks

Stock markets (including NASDAQ and the registered exchanges, such as the NYSE or AMEX) have specific requirements that the companies listed there must meet. The companies may have to have a certain amount of revenue or a stock price over a set level or have been in existence for a certain amount of time. These requirements are strictly monitored and enforced. You will occasionally hear of a stock being delisted, which means that the stock stopped meeting one or more of the requirements and has been removed from the exchange. Companies listed on a stock market have to meet certain obligations in terms of reporting. both for frequency and amount of detail.

Companies that do not meet the requirements for listing on a major exchange have the option of offering unlisted securities that trade *over the counter,* or OTC. There are established OTC quotation systems such as the OTC Bulletin Board (OTCBB) or the Pink Sheets. It is important to realize that these quotation services are exactly that—places that list prices to buy or sell a stock—rather than organizations with the responsibility for monitoring a company and its situation.

The OTCBB and the Pink Sheets differ in important

ways. First, the NASDAQ operates the OTCBB service and permits members of the National Association of Securities Dealers (NASD) to quote a buying or selling price on any OTC security that is up to date with certain required regulatory filings. The Pink Sheets is a privately owned company that allows NASD members to provide prices on any OTC security and does not maintain any regulatory filing requirements. An OTC security can be quoted on both the OTCBB and the Pink Sheets.

Think of the price listing system as analogous to the classified ads in your local newspaper. An ad might be for the sale of a used car or a piece of sports equipment, but the newspaper is not going to take responsibility that the car or baseball bat is in good condition. The paper does not inspect every item, and the buyer takes the risk that something is not as advertised.

The filing requirements and other standards that companies must meet to be listed on the major exchanges are helpful to individual investors, especially with international stocks. As I have said before, investing in international stocks is just like buying stocks in U.S. companies. It is important in both cases to reduce the risk of investing by learning what you can about the company, its management, and its operations. The organization of relevant information into periodic reports makes getting this information much easier. The fact that a company has been willing to subject itself to the requirements and oversight of a major exchange should make you feel better about investing in the company.

Finding Information on Stocks

It is quite easy to find information on stocks anywhere in the world. The challenge is in finding reliable information that you can understand. One of the benefits of investing in U.S.-listed stocks is that a lot of information is available for free and in English.

If you have read something in the newspaper or a magazine or learned about a trend that you want to try to invest in, one easy place to start looking for information about that trend is on the Internet. Through your own Internet connection or one available for free at a library or for a small fee at an Internet cafe, you can find lots of information about a trend and the investment opportunities available to play that trend.

Say, for example, that you heard that car sales in China have been strong recently. Typing "car sales China" into Google or AltaVista will produce over 15 million sites you can visit to find information on this topic. Searching the news available on the Web for the same topic provides over 1,200 recent news stories that refer to car sales in China.

A quick scan of the top stories reveals that Volkswagen has been enjoying strong car sales recently and that its joint-venture partners in China are First Automotive Works Corp. and Shanghai Automotive Industry Corp. Another story tells you that the government is planning to raise the tax rate on larger cars at the end of the year. A quick read of the tax article reveals that

Volkswagon

Country: Germany	Sector: (Automobiles		
US Ticker	Price as of 2/21/06	52-week range:	Dividend:	Yield:
VLKAY.PK	$59.75	$64.2-$41.9	$1.15	0.0%

COMPANY DESCRIPTION

Volkswagen AG (the Volkswagen Group) is an automobile manufacturer and a car producer in Europe. It consists of the Volkswagen plants in Wolfsburg, Brunswick, Hanover, Kassel, Emden and Salzgitter. It is the parent company of all other companies in the Volkswagen Group, which are either wholly owned subsidiaries or companies in which Volkswagen AG has majority ownership. The Company operates 44 production plants in 11 European countries, as well as seven countries in the Americas, Asia and Africa. The Volkswagen Group sells its vehicles in more than 150 countries.

SALES AND EARNINGS (in millions, except per-share data)

FY ends:	Sales	EBITDA	Pre-Tax Profit	Net Profit	EPS	CF/S	Div.	Sales Growth	EBITDA Margin	Pre-tax Margin	ROE
12/08E	100,777	12,978	3,280	n/a	5.12	25.61	1.57	2.1%	12.9%	3.3%	
12/07E	98,694	11,441	3,218	n/a	4.98	24.58	1.37	2.7%	11.6%	3.3%	
12/06A	96,122	10,178	2,100	n/a	3.53	23.13	1.22	0.9%	10.6%	2.2%	
12/05A	95,268	n/a	1,722	112m	n/a	n/a	n/a	7.1%	n/a	1.8%	
12/04A	88,963	n/a	1,099	716m	n/a	n/a	n/a	n/a	n/a	1.2%	

Average Growth Rates:

	Sales	EBITDA	Pre-Tax Profit	Net Profit	EPS	CF/S	Div.
05-07E	2%	13%	25%	n/a	21%	5%	14%
04-05A	7%	n/a	57%	n/a	n/a	n/a	n/a

VALUATION

P/E 12/08E	11.7x	Price/Book	0.7x
P/E 12/07E	17.3x	FV/EBITDA 12/07E	11.6
Price/Revs 12/07E	0.2x	P/CFLO per share	1.99

SHARE DATA

Market cap (US$ mil.)	27,451	Avg. Daily Vol. (000)	4,599
Primary shares (mil.)	320.29m	Avg. Daily Vol. ($ mn)	$ 271
Float (mil.)	n/a	Institutional ownership	27%
		Insider ownership	49%

KEY RATIOS (%)

BALANCE SHEET SUMMARY (as of 6/30/05)

Current assets	60,465	Current Liabilities	54,960
Fixed assets	73,793	Long-term debt	31,330
Other assets	0	Other liabilities	22,915
		Equity	25,053
Total assets	134,258	Total liab.s & equity	134,258
		L-T Debt/Capital	23.3%

RIEDEL
RESEARCH GROUP INC OBJECTIVE EQUITY RESEARCH

Exhibit 2.1 Volkswagen
(Riedel Research Group, data from Reuters)

Brilliance China Automotive Holdings Ltd

Country: China	Sector: Automotive		
US Ticker	Price as of 2/21/06	52-week range:	Dividend:	Yield:
CBA	$18.72	$22.72-$12.67		0.0%

COMPANY DESCRIPTION

Brilliance China is a Chinese company principally engaged in manufacturing and sale of minibuses and automotive components.

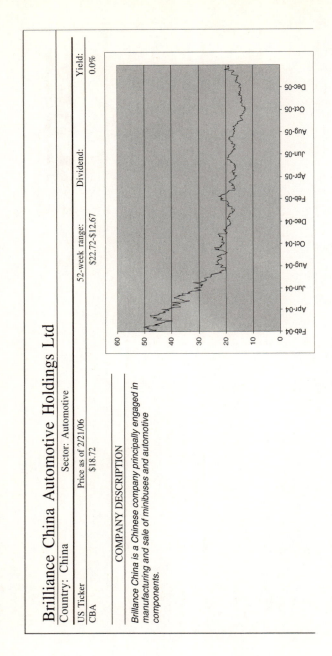

SALES AND EARNINGS (in millions, except per-share data)

FY ends:	Sales	EBITDA	Pre-Tax Profit	Net Profit	EPS	CF/S	Div.	Sales Growth	EBITDA Margin	Pre-tax Margin	ROE
12/07E	1,106	n/a	n/a	n/a	0.24	n/a	0.00	14.9%	n/a'a	n/a	n/a
12/06E	963	n/a	n/a	n/a	0.24	n/a	0.00	54.2%	n/a'a	n/a	n/a
12/05A	624	n/a	n/a	n/a	0.99	n/a	0.00	-90.5%	n/a'a	n/a	n/a
12/04A	6,542	n/a	450	407.8	n/a	n/a	0.00	-35.3%	n/a	6.9%	13.6%
12/03A #	10,110	n/a	1,253	1,099.0	n/a	n/a	0.00	n/a	n/a	12.4%	0.7%

KEY RATIOS (%)

Average Growth Rates:

	Sales	EBITDA	Pre-Tax Profit	Net Profit	EPS	CF/S
05-07E	33%	n/a	n/a	n/a	-51%	n/a
03-05A	n/a	n/a	n/a	n/a	n/a	n/a

VALUATION

P/E 12/07E	78.0x	Price/Book	0.8x
P/E 12/06E	78.0x	FV/EBITDA 12/06E	48.4
Price/Revs 12/06E	0.8x	P/CFLO per share	-456

SHARE DATA

Market cap (US$ mil.)	685	Avg. Daily Vol. (000)	46340
Primary shares (mil.)	36.7	Avg. Daily Vol. ($ mm)	0.83
Float (mil.)	n/a	Institutional ownership	2.0%
		Insider ownership	0.0%

BALANCE SHEET SUMMARY (as of 6/30/05)

Current assets	8,034	Current Liabilities	7,116
Fixed assets	8,085	Long-term debt	1,511
Other assets	0	Other liabilities	790
		Equity	6,702
Total assets	16,119	Total liab.s & equity	16,119
		L-T Debt/Capital	9.4%

RIEDEL
RESEARCH GROUP INC OBJECTIVE EQUITY RESEARCH

Exhibit 2.2 Brilliance China
(Riedel Research Group, data from Reuters)

the increased tax rate applies mainly to imported cars with much larger engines than those that Volkswagen is selling.

So how do you invest in the fact that Volkswagen is having good sales in China? You could buy Volkswagen stock. A quick search of Yahoo!Finance (www.yahoo .com) tells you that shares in this German company trade on the German markets and in London and that there is an ADR available in New York. It is this ADR that allows an individual investor to conveniently participate in Volkswagen's growth. The ADR trades on the NYSE as VLKAY and can be bought just like any stock. Looking at the Bank of New York ADR web site (www.bnyadr.com) tells you that VLKAY was a good investment in 2005 and was up more than 30 percent. See Exhibit 2.1.

The issue with buying the Volkswagen ADR is that you are not getting exposure just to their sales in China but also to the success of their various brands around the world. You may want to buy into Volkswagen's sales worldwide, but you may prefer to find something more directly related to the Chinese auto market.

Back on Yahoo!Finance, you find that the companies listed as Volkswagen's partners in China (First Automotive Works Corp. and Shanghai Automotive Industry Corp.) do not appear to be listed. But there are other Chinese auto companies that are listed—lots of them. China Automotive Systems, a steering system manufacturer in China, is listed on the NASDAQ (under ticker CAAS). Brilliance China Automotive, a Chinese auto

parts and engine manufacturer and a joint-venture partner of BMW in China, offers an ADR that trades on the
NYSE under ticker CBA. See Exhibit 2.2.

Through Yahoo!Finance, Bloomberg.com, and other
free financial sites, you can learn pretty much anything
you want to know about these stocks. Who is the management? How has the company's profitability been?
How much revenue and profit were reported in the last
quarter? Last year? What are analysts expecting for earnings next year? How do the profitability and performance
of the company compare with those of other automotive companies? Because of the U.S. listings, both companies release frequent and detailed reports about their
business and how they are doing financially. All the
information you need to decide whether this is a stock
you would like to buy is available.

The next question is: How reliable is this information?

Disclosure Requirements and Reporting Standards

The fact that U.S.-listed companies must regularly provide press releases and financial information in English
is one of the central reasons that such direct listings and
ADRs are a good way to invest in these companies.
These filings and the information they provide go a long
way toward helping you make an investment decision.
Can they be trusted?

Shares of foreign companies listed directly on a U.S.

exchange must meet all the same requirements as a U.S. company listed there. The company has to provide quarterly financial reports (10-Qs) and annual financial reports (10-Ks), and it must report important information quickly after it happens (usually in a press release and a filing called an 8-K). The SEC requires that companies have qualified auditors reviewing and approving their financial statements. These auditors must state categorically that every set of financial documents issued as "audited" has, in fact, been properly reviewed by the auditing firm, and they must sign off on every set of financial reports. In fact, since 1977, all companies filing reports with the SEC have had to have in place systems of checks and balances throughout their company to ensure that accurate and appropriate financial information is being collected and reported.

Companies with ADRs that trade in the United States must provide the SEC with at least all of the documents that their home market requires. So if France requires that its companies provide financial results at least every six months, then those same documents must be provided to the SEC and made available to the investing public. If Poland requires quarterly statements, then those same quarterly statements have to be made available to U.S. investors.

In fact, many of the companies with ADRs in the United States provide reports that are above and beyond what they file in their own countries. Having more frequent updates on a company and its prospects is helpful. More information more frequently is always a good thing.

The issue of trusting financial reports is a tough one for U.S. investors. Having had their confidence shaken by scandals at major companies such as Enron, WorldCom, and HealthSouth, investors have become very skeptical of whatever a company is telling them. The same caution should be applied to international companies. There have been a number of scandals in international companies as well in recent years, including Parmalat, Hollinger, and China Aviation Oil.

Sarbanes-Oxley

Following the corporate scandals of Enron, WorldCom, and other U.S.-listed companies in the late 1990s, government regulators wanted to find a way to make the information provided by companies to their investors more reliable. It is vitally important to the investment process and the integrity of markets to have the best information possible available to assess risk, opportunity, and value. Only by having accurate information can an investor begin to assess the value of a possible investment.

The approach that the SEC took was to require more outside supervision of the information collected, a stronger role for the company's board of directors, and more personal responsibility from the executives of the company. On an annual basis, the auditor conducting the audit must state that the company has adequate "internal control" to ensure that the information being collected on the company's operations and finances is a true and proper reflection of the company's performance and condition. This is a fancy way of saying that the auditor has to be able to say that the right information is being collected and reported. In addition, the chief executive officer (CEO) and chief financial officer (CFO) must sign statements that they have reviewed the report (whether for a quarter or for a year) and that, based on their knowledge, it does not contain any untrue statement of a material fact or omit anything material. The idea of this personal certification is to make the executives think twice about whether the information contained in the statements is a true and accurate reflection of what they know about the condition of the company. It also makes it easier to sue these people if it turns out that there was something inaccurate in the statements and they knew it. There are also requirements that if financial statements later prove to be inaccurate, the executives must give back compensation earned during the period in question. Talk about hitting them where it hurts!

The requirements of Sarbanes-Oxley, with which most companies must comply in 2006 or 2007, have been the subject of considerable debate because many smaller listed companies have complained about the added expense of adhering to these requirements. From the investor's point of view, however, any improvement

Of course, Sarbanes-Oxley is no panacea for the ills in the equity market. Any CEO or CFO who is going to deceive investors is not going to have too much trouble lying to them again by certifying false statements. The threat of jail time and the fear of being personally culpable might make someone think twice, but a fraud is always a fraud. As I write this book at the end of 2005, we just witnessed one of the most spectacular implosions of a Wall Street firm in recent history. Refco, one of the leading commodities brokerages and commodities finance houses, rapidly went to pieces when it was discovered that the CEO had been lying to investors. It turns out that the Sarbanes-Oxley legislation contains a huge loophole. Companies don't have to file Sarbanes-Oxley disclaimers and statements with their initial public offerings (IPOs). Refco went public to great acclaim just two short months prior to this scandal. These troubles came to light when the company went to file its first quarterly report. What a disaster!

Unfortunately, as is too often the case in situations like this, clear signs that there was something wrong—or least warnings that there might be something wrong—were very evident in the months and years before the IPO. A number of the companies that Refco had acquired had previously experienced problems with the regulators. There were plenty of stories being circulated about the NASD or SEC having investigated these companies. (Chapter 7 discusses this subject in more detail.) My advice to you if you catch wind of legal trouble at a company you own: Run!

in the reliability of information about a company is welcome.

Foreign companies and executives have complained that Sarbanes-Oxley is hard to comply with because of the particular situation in their home countries with the auditing firms they work with. They have also complained about the cost of compliance. The Sarbanes-Oxley requirements apply to companies that are directly listed on any of the U.S. exchanges. Remember that these companies are just like any other listed company; their operations and headquarters just happen to be overseas. The requirements also apply to many, but not all, of the ADRs that we previously discussed.

So How Good Is the Information? Usually Pretty Good

The important thing to remember is that the information provided on the investment opportunities in international companies listed in the United States is not perfect, but it is usually quite good. The information is reviewed by professional accountants (auditors) and, while not flawless, is usually reliable. A warning: If there is ever even a whiff of concern about the quality and accuracy of information provided (especially the announcement of a review by the SEC), get out of the stock and move on to something else. There are plenty of other companies to invest in, and the old adage usually applies: "Where there is smoke, there is fire." I recommend selling and moving on to something else.

So, there are lots of international companies to invest in. These ADRs and direct listings trade in U.S. dollars and are just as easy to buy as securities from U.S. companies like Microsoft, IBM, and Coca-Cola. These stocks have a place in your portfolio to help your investments keep pace with the globalization taking place in all other parts of your life.

Which ones do I buy and how do I put together an appropriate portfolio of international stocks? The next few chapters will discuss how to put together a group (or portfolio) of these stocks, how to find stocks that provide exposure to the trends that you are excited about, and how to assess the risk and opportunity of these stocks. One of the first things we will discuss is diversification. If you own lots of different unrelated things, chances are that one disappointment or surprise will not ruin the value of your portfolio. By diversifying, you reduce the impact of any one company on your portfolio. The other benefit of a diversified portfolio is that you have a number of interesting companies to follow and pay attention to. Remember, this is supposed to be fun as well as profitable.

Chapter THREE

Diversify—Don't Put All Your Eggs in One Basket

Diversify by Region, Country, and Company

Don't put all your eggs in one basket. This commonsense statement is especially important when you are investing your money. You should invest in a number of different things so that if one of them goes bad (i.e., down in value), you do not lose all of your money. The beauty of diversification is that you can improve the performance of your investments while reducing the risk. Clearly, there is no free lunch, but reducing the risk and improving the return is always preferable. Investing internationally is, you will see, an important part of diversifying your portfolio. Luckily, diversification is quite easy to achieve when you are investing overseas because you can invest in many different companies, industries, countries, and situations that are not related to one another.

Company Risk and Market Risk

It is important to understand the different types of risk that you face when you own a portfolio of stocks. There is company risk and market risk.

Company risk is the risk that the particular company in which you are investing will fall down for some reason. The company might be weak relative to competitors or the particular technology that it uses might be surpassed by something else. Imagine a pharmaceutical company that relies on one particular drug for much of its profit. If that drug proves to be ineffective or even dangerous, shares in that company are going to fall. If another pharmaceutical company comes out with a drug that treats the same illness or symptom but does so more effectively, shares in the company being surpassed are going to fall.

Changes in technology can likewise be a source of company risk. Being the best maker of buggy whips is not going to help you if everyone is starting to buy cars. The same holds true for creators of computer technology, advertising firms that specialize in a certain type of advertising, and manufacturers that face competition from cheaper producers. Furthermore, you might encounter a situation where a company is simply poorly run or managed or perhaps one where fraud is involved. The disasters at WorldCom, Enron, and Refco were specific to those companies, and if you had stock in those companies, you paid the price. However, the frauds at those companies did not mean that every telecom, energy, or commodities company was crooked and failing. In fact, some of the competitors in those industries benefited from the demise of a major company in the same business. All those WorldCom customers had to find a new telecom service provider, and quickly.

The easiest way to avoid company-specific risk is to buy stock in a few different companies in an industry you like. If you think Japanese banks are turning around and that business is going to be good for them for a while, buy stock in a few different ones so that you are betting on the direction of the industry or sector rather than on the fortunes of one particular bank or management team. By buying shares in Mitsubishi UFJ Financial Group (MTU), Sumitomo Trust and Banking (STBUY), and Bank of Yokohama (BKJAY), you are betting on the Japanese banking sector rather than on one particular company. If one of the companies turns out to be poorly run or a victim of fraud, it is unlikely to contaminate the other companies and stocks. Buying stock in a number of different companies reduces your exposure to one company's bad luck.

There can be risk in a group of companies because something might happen that would impact the sector as a whole. In the Japanese bank example, a change in lending regulations or interest rates might be good or bad for the entire industry. All of the bank stocks are going to rise or fall as a result—some more than others, probably, but they will move in the same direction if something changes for the whole industry.

Market risk is the second type of risk. This is the risk that something will hit all stocks at the same time. Events such as the terrorist attacks of September 11, 2001, the impact of higher oil prices on inflation and consumers, political unrest, and an increase in interest rates impact all companies. In the Japanese bank example, the market risk relates to something happening to the country of Japan that has an impact on how investors envision what is going to happen to the country or on the outlook for business there. No matter how many different stocks you own, if all stocks are going down, your stocks are going to go down as well.

Having investments in different companies reduces your risk. Having investments in different industries reduces your risk. And having investments in different countries really reduces your risk. The Japanese bank example is a good illustration of this. As we have seen, owning stock in a few different Japanese banks helps reduce company-specific risk (the bad luck of a particular company). Owning stock in Japanese banks as well as in Japanese oil companies helps to reduce the risk that a particular sector will get hurt. Owning stock in banks in Japan as well as banks in Korea or Singapore or France, Germany, or Australia reduces the impact that a significant development in the Japanese banking sector would have on your portfolio.

Without getting too technical, it is important at this point to introduce the concept of correlation. *Correlation* is the way that events interact. It is a measure of the historical tendency of two things to happen together. In simple words, correlation is the tendency of one thing to "zig" when another thing "zags" or for two things to "zig" together. If every time GM shares go up, Ford shares go up as well, then these two are highly correlated. If every time Microsoft shares go up, Apple computer shares go down, they are also highly correlated. Note that there is a high correlation even when the movement is in opposite directions.

Back to the idea of not putting your eggs in one basket: You do not get much value from investing in a set of things that are highly correlated. If your stocks are all going to go up or down together, you are not benefiting much from diversification. If half of your stocks go up in a tight relationship to the other half going down, then you are never going to get anywhere.

Correlations are measured by the *correlation coefficient*, which is a number between −1 and 1 that defines the degree of correlation between two things. Table 3.1 shows the way correlation coefficients work.

Big companies like IBM, Coca-Cola, Microsoft, and Citigroup trade much the same as the overall U.S. stock market. Thinking of the S&P 500 Index as a pretty good approximation of the overall market, if the S&P 500 goes up by 5 percent, chances are that these big companies will go up by something like 5 percent. This means that these stocks are very correlated to the S&P 500.

Table 3.1

Correlation Coefficient	Interaction
1	They go up exactly the same amount—if one goes up by 5%, the other goes up by 5%.
0.5	They go in the same direction, but not exactly the same amount.
0	There is no relationship at all.
−0.5	They move in opposite directions, but not the same amount.
−1.0	They move exactly the same amount in opposite directions. If one goes up 5%, the other goes down 5%.

Just as there are relationships in how companies trade relative to the U.S. market, there are relationships in how international markets trade relative to the U.S. market and relative to each other.

Over the past 31 years, the correlation between U.S. and international markets has averaged 0.5 (source: SSgA, International Diversification, July 15, 2005). This correlation has varied over time between 0.1 and 0.8. In the period between 1980 and 2003, for example, the correlation between the S&P 500 and foreign stocks (as measured by the MSCI EAFE Index) was 0.7 (source: Alliance Bernstein *Fortune or Misfortune*, June 2004, www.alliancebernstein.com).

How Much Diversification Is Too Much?

The risk with too much diversification, however, is that you are not getting exposure to the particular theme that you are trying to invest in. If you really believe in the Japanese banking system, then the right way to play that theme is by buying into a few different banks in that market. If you spread your investment over banks in a bunch of different countries, you reduce the benefit to your portfolio when you are proven right about the Japanese banking sector and the Japanese bank stock double. If you want to make a bet on the direction of the banking sector in Asia, then buy into Asian banks. If you want to bet on Japanese banks, then buy into Japanese banks. The trick is to be playing a number of different themes at the same time. If you are betting on the improvement in Japanese banks as well as the future of Turkey as a member of the European Union and the outlook for minerals being mined in Africa, you have a well-diversified portfolio. By investing in a few plays on each of these themes, you have global diversification, industry diversification, company diversification, and an interesting set of companies that you own a stake in to learn about, track, and, hopefully, make money from.

I will use some of the themes I am thinking about as an example of diversification in your portfolio. These are not investment recommendations, but they are intended to illustrate what you might put together to build a strong, diversified, and profitable portfolio for yourself.

Remember that by the time this book comes out, these themes will likely not be appropriate. They will have already played out and the world situation will have changed. This is meant to be an illustration, not a guide. This book and this chapter aim to provide you with tools, not investment ideas. Please take these tools and apply them to your interests during a particular time in which you're investing and in your particular situation.

Three Sample Investment Themes

The three themes that I am considering in late 2005 are (1) oil prices stay high, (2) Japan's economy finally recovers, and (3) Latin America enters a strong phase of export-led growth. These are plausible themes that would be interesting for someone to consider, investigate, and invest in. They are diversified in terms of companies, region, and focus, and they are not very correlated.

Theme 1: Oil Prices Stay High

Oil prices have been rising in recent years. This fact has provided a number of challenges to economies around the world, but has also provided some interesting investing opportunities.

As you can see in Figures 3.1 and 3.2, an FTSE

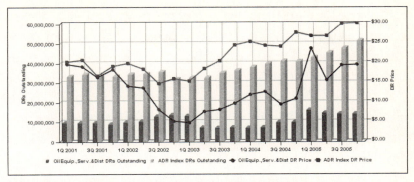

Figure 3.1 Oil Equipment, Service, and Distribution versus
ADR Index
(DRs Outstanding and DR Price)

(Financial Times Stock Exchange) Index of oil and gas
companies was up by 55 percent from April 2002
through October 2005. To put that performance in perspective, the Dow Jones Index was up less than 2 percent over the same period.

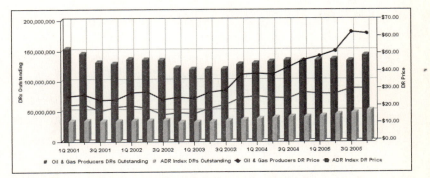

Figure 3.2 Oil and Gas Producers versus ADR Index
(DRs Outstanding and DR Price)

Note as well that the correlation of the FTSE Index of oil and gas companies to the price of a barrel of oil is very high as the value of global oil companies moves in tandem with the price of a barrel of oil.

A quick search of the Bank of New York ADR web site (www.bnyadr.com) shows that there are 76 international oil and gas producing stocks that you can buy in the United States to get exposure to oil and gas prices and play the theme of oil prices staying high.

Looking at the various options, I select China Petroleum & Chemical (SNP), British Petroleum (BP), Russian player LukOil (LUK), and Argentine company Petrobras (PZE). Note that I have chosen companies in various markets and regions, but all are related to oil and gas.

Dividing your investment among these four stocks gives you exposure to high oil prices while limiting your exposure to the possibility of one particular country or company going bad. This can be very risky. For example, going though this exercise a few years ago, you might have considered investing in the Russian oil company Yukos. The financials of the company looked fine, the exposure to rapid growth in Russian oil looked solid, and there was no reason (at first glance) to avoid investing in the company. However, over the calendar year 2004 you would have lost 95 percent of the value of your investment. What happened was that the head of the company started funding political parties in opposition to President Vladimir Putin. This turned out to be a bad idea. Yukos head Mikhail Khodorkovsky ended up in jail on tax charges, and the company was broken up and sold for a song to comrades of President Putin.

As you'll learn in Chapter 7, this is a perfect example of an avoidable loss if you apply the rule of always knowing the shareholders in a company you are buying. You have to watch for the signs that something has changed. In this case, it was a hard hint to miss—the head of the company was arrested on October 25, 2003. At the time of his arrest, Yukos shares traded at $46. This was all before the precipitous drop in the share price to the $2 to $3 level. In a situation like this, when the head of a company is arrested, you should sell your shares. It is not likely that things will go well for the hapless executive in the face of a powerful leader like Putin in a country like Russia. Think about it: What is your upside? Are the shares going to double from where they are with the corporate head in jail on tax charges and the government doing everything it can to attack this company? Are the odds in Khodorkovsky's favor or against him? Are they in your favor? I think not. I say, sell your shares and move to something else. There are too many opportunities all over the world to worry about staying exposed to one particular stock that has run afoul of a strong government and is at the mercy of a determined government machine.

Returning to the oil idea, I have identified a theme (oil prices are going to stay high), used the Bank of New York ADR site (www.bnyadr.com) to find a diverse group

China Petroleum and Chemical Corp (Sinopec)

Country: China	Sector: Oil and Gas		
US Ticker	Price as of 02/21/06	52-week range:	Dividend:	Yield:
SNP	$59.59	$63.73-$35.55	$0.97	0.0%

COMPANY DESCRIPTION

The company engages in explore for, develop, and produce crude oil and natural gas, refining, distribution and marketing of gasoline, diesel, jet fuel and most other refined products, and production and distribution of petrochemicals in China.

SALES AND EARNINGS (in millions, except per-share data)								KEY RATIOS (%)			
			Pre-Tax	Net				Sales	EBITDA	Pre-tax	
FY ends:	Sales	EBITDA	Profit	Profit	EPS	CF/S	Div.	Growth	Margin	Margin	ROE
12/07E	93,767	13,846	8,551	n/a	5.58	n/a	1.71	-2.4%	14.8%	9.1%	n/a
12/06E	96,059	13,548	8,599	n/a	6.81	n/a	1.71	6.3%	14.1%	9.0%	n/a
12/05A	90,342	11,975	8,070	n/a	5.64	n/a	0.98	37.0%	13.3%	8.9%	17.3%
12/04A	65,931	n/a	6,529	3,936	n/a	n/a	0.73	29.6%	n/a	9.9%	n/a
12/03A	50,877	n/a	3,660	2,318	n/a	n/a	0.73	n/a	n/a	7.2%	n/a
Average Growth Rates:											
05-07E	2%	8%	3%	n/a	-1%						
03-05A	30%	n/a	78%	70%	n/a						

VALUATION			
P/E 12/07E	10.6x	Price/Book	0.4x
P/E 12/06E	11.4x	FV/EBITDA 12/06E	6.2
Price/Revs 12/06E	0.1x	P/CFLO per share	n/a

BALANCE SHEET SUMMARY (as of 6/30/05)			
Current assets	135,315	Current Liabilities	151,747
Fixed assets	357,671	Long-term debt	113,599
Other assets	0	Other liabilities	30,069
		Equity	197,571
Total assets	492,986	Total liab.s & equity	492,986
		L-T Debt/Capital	23.0%

SHARE DATA			
Market cap (US$ mil.)	53,929	Avg. Daily Vol. (000)	0.21m
Primary shares (mil.)	167.8	Avg. Daily Vol. ($ mn)	$ 12
Float (mil.)	n/a	Institutional ownership	41.0%
		Insider ownership	3.5%

RIEDEL RESEARCH GROUP INC OBJECTIVE EQUITY RESEARCH

Exhibit 3.1 China Petroleum and Chemical Corp.
(Riedel Research Group, data from Reuters)

British Petroleum

Country: UK		Sector: Oil and Gas		
US Ticker	Price as of 02/21/06	52-week range:	Dividend:	Yield:
BP	$67.38	$72.31-$58.45	$2.25	3.3%

COMPANY DESCRIPTION

BP p.l.c. is an oil company with three main businesses: Exploration and Production; Gas, Power and Renewables, and Refining and Marketing. Exploration and Production includes oil and natural gas exploration and field development and production, together with pipeline transportation and natural gas processing. Gas, Power and Renewables activities include marketing and trading of natural gas, natural gas liquid, new market development, liquefied natural gas and solar and renewables. The activities of Refining and Marketing include oil supply and trading, as well as refining and marketing. In September 2003, BP merged its Russian assets into those of Tyumen Oil Co. (TNK), creating TNK-BP, a joint venture between the Company and the Alfa Group and Access-Renova (collectively, AAR). In addition, the Company plans to incorporate AAR's 50% interest in OAO Slavneft, a Russian oil company, into TNK-BP.

46

SALES AND EARNINGS (in millions, except per-share data) — KEY RATIOS (%)

FY ends:	Sales	EBITDA	Pre-tax Profit	Net Profit	EPS	CF/S	Div.	Sales Growth	EBITDA Margin	Pre-tax Margin	ROE
12/08E	229,956	n/a	8,291	n/a	5.21	n/a	2.58	-24.8%	n/a	3.6%	n/a
12/07E	305,691	n/a	7,764	n/a	7.06	n/a	2.38	4.1%	n/a	2.5%	n/a
12/06E	293,531	n/a	7,759	n/a	6.68	n/a	2.21	17.7%	n/a	2.6%	17.3%
12/05A	249,465	n/a	6,034	n/a	6.34	n/a	n/a	-12.5%	n/a	2.4%	n/a
12/04A	285,059	n/a	2,269	n/a	4.32	n/a	n/a	n/a	n/a	0.8%	n/a

Average Growth Rates:

	Sales	EBITDA	Pre-tax Profit	EPS	CF/S
06-08E	-11%	n/a	3%	-12%	n/a
04-05A	-12%	n/a	166%	n/a	n/a

VALUATION

P/E 12/08E	12.9x	Price/Book	3.2x
P/E 12/07E	10.8x	FV/EBITDA 12/07E	8.1
Price/Revs 12/07E	0.9x	P/CFLO per share	61.65

BALANCE SHEET SUMMARY (as of 6/30/05)

Current assets	75,290	Current Liabilities	71,497
Fixed assets	131,624	Long-term debt	10,230
Other assets	0	Other liabilities	45,221
		Equity	79,976
Total assets	206,914	Total liab.s & equity	206,914
		L-T Debt/Capital	4.9%

SHARE DATA

Market cap (US$ mil.)	231,388	Avg. Daily Vol. (000)	4.48m
Primary shares (mil.)	3,587.7	Avg. Daily Vol. ($ mn)	$ 302
Float (mil.)	n/a	Institutional ownership	51.0%
		Insider ownership	8.0%

RIEDEL
RESEARCH GROUP INC OBJECTIVE EQUITY RESEARCH

Exhibit 3.2 · British Petroleum
(Riedel Research Group, data from Reuters)

47

LukOil Holding

Country: Russia		Sector: Oil and Gas

US Ticker	Price as of 02/21/06		
LUKOF.PK	$79.00		

52-week range:	Dividend:	Yield:
$80.4 - $28.8	$1.35	0.0%

COMPANY DESCRIPTION

Lukoil is engaged in oil and gas production, oil refining and petrochemical production. The Company operates in 40 regions in Russia and 25 countries worldwide. The Company runs the LUKTrans-Shipping and OAO LUKOIL-Arktik-Tanker shipping companies.

SALES AND EARNINGS (in millions, except per-share data)

| | | | Pre-Tax | Net | | | | | KEY RATIOS (%) | | |
| | | | | | | | | Sales | EBITDA | Pre-tax | |
FY ends:	Sales	EBITDA	Profit	Profit	EPS	CF/S	Div.	Growth	Margin	Margin	ROE
12/07E	54,634	9,573	8,530	n/a	6.89	6.94	1.73	-3.6%	17.5%	15.6%	n/a
12/06E	56,674	9,457	7,884	n/a	7.03	9.59	1.61	6.7%	16.7%	13.9%	n/a
12/05A	53,122	9,537	8,386	n/a	7.18	8.76	1.41	55.9%	18.0%	15.8%	17.3%
12/04A	34,068	6,284	6,070	4,310	n/a	n/a	n/a	n/a	18.4%	17.8%	n/a
12/03A	n/a	n/a	n/a	n/a	n/a	n/a	n/a	n/a	n/a	n/a	n/a

Average Growth Rates:

	Sales	EBITDA	Pre-Tax Profit	Net Profit	EPS	CF/S
05-07E	1%	0%	1%	n/a	-2%	-11%
04-05A	56%	52%	38%	n/a	n/a	n/a

VALUATION

P/E 12/07E	11.5x	Price/Book	1.3x
P/E 12/06E	6.3x	FV/EBITDA 12/06E	9.8
Price/Revs 12/06E	0.8x	P/CFLO per share	9.02

BALANCE SHEET SUMMARY (as of 6/30/05)

Current assets	8,574	Current Liabilities	4,545
Fixed assets	21,187	Long-term debt	2,609
Other assets	0	Other liabilities	1,796
		Equity	20,811
Total assets	29,761	Total liab.s & equity	29,761
		L-T Debt/Capital	8.8%

SHARE DATA

Market cap (US$ mil.)	66,612	Avg. Daily Vol. (000)	0.47m
Primary shares (mil.)	850.6	Avg. Daily Vol. ($ mm)	$ 37.1
Float (mil.)	n/a	Institutional ownership	1.5%
		Insider ownership	19.5%

RIEDEL RESEARCH GROUP INC OBJECTIVE EQUITY RESEARCH

Exhibit 3.3 LukOil
(Riedel Research Group, data from Reuters)

49

Petrobras

Country: Argentina   Sector: Energy

US Ticker	Price as of 02/21/06	52-week range:	Dividend:	Yield:
PZE	$11.70	$16.28-$10.95		0.0%

COMPANY DESCRIPTION

Petrobras Energia Representaciones S.A. is an investment company owning 98% of Petrobras Energia S.A.The main business of Petrobras Energia is the petroleum and natural gas exploration and production in Argentina and other Latin American countries. This company is controlled by the brazilian Petrobras S.A.

SALES AND EARNINGS (in millions, except per-share data)

FY ends:	Sales	EBITDA	Net Income	Shares (mil.)	EPS	FCF/S	Div.	KEY RATIOS (%) EBITDA Margin	Tax Rate	Net Margin	ROE
12/06E	11,228	4,502	1,178	2,132	0.55	0.48	0.00	40.1%	26.2%	10.5%	12.5%
12/05E	9,450	3,955	835	2,132	0.39	0.40	0.00	41.9%	31.5%	8.8%	12.2%
12/04A	6,974	2,789	678	2,132	0.32	0.20	0.00	40.0%	-38.2%	9.7%	12.3%
12/03A	5,494	2,248	381	2,132	0.18	0.25	0.00	40.9%	3.2%	6.9%	7.9%
12/02A	5,106	2,178	-1,579	2,132	(0.74)	0.02	0.00	42.7%	36.9%	-30.9%	-35.5%

Average Growth Rates:

	Sales	EBITDA	Net Income	Shares	EPS
05-06E	19%	14%	41%	0%	41%
02-05A	23%	22%	n/a	0%	n/a

VALUATION

P/E 12/06E	Price/Book	1.4x
P/E 12/05E	FV/EBITDA 12/05E	
Price/Revs 12/05E	P/CFLO per share	

BALANCE SHEET SUMMARY (as of 6/30/05)

Current assets	1m	Current Liabilities	21m
Fixed assets	5482m	Long-term debt	0
Other assets	0	Other liabilities	(49)
		Equity	5511m
Total assets	5483m	Total liab.s & equity	5483m
		L-T Debt/Capital	0.0%

SHARE DATA

Market cap (US$ mil.)	2,558	Avg. Daily Vol. (000)	0.10m
Primary shares (mil.)	213.2	Avg. Daily Vol. ($ mn)	$ 1.17
Float (mil.)	n/a	Institutional ownership	3.0%
		Insider ownership	0.0%

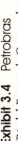

RIEDEL
RESEARCH GROUP INC OBJECTIVE EQUITY RESEARCH

Exhibit 3.4 Petrobras
(Riedel Research Group, data from Reuters)

of stocks to get exposure to the theme, and, by diversifying across countries and companies, I have invested in the theme without being too exposed to one company's bad luck. The Yukos example in Russia illustrated one company's very bad luck. There was plenty of warning about the risk in the Yukos story well before the stock price collapsed. Remember the rules: Know the shareholders, and if things get complicated, sell and move on to the next opportunity. See Exhibits 3.1 through 3.4.

Theme 2: Japan's Economy Finally Recovers

Japan is the second-largest economy in the world after the United States. Given the prevalence worldwide of Japanese products (automobiles, electronics, and computers are just a few examples), it would be naïve to ignore the power of the Japanese economy. It would have been exceptionally naïve, however, to invest in the power of the Japanese economy over the past few years. Between 1990 and the year 2000, the Japanese stock market declined by 65 percent. In a market that is declining that much and that broadly, it is very hard to make money, no matter how careful you are in picking your stocks. In the last 6 to 12 months, however, the Japanese economy and market have started to show signs of life. The Japan Index was up 40 percent in the second half of 2005, and many people are talking about the long-awaited recovery in the Japanese economy. See Figure 3.3

One of the things that happened to change market

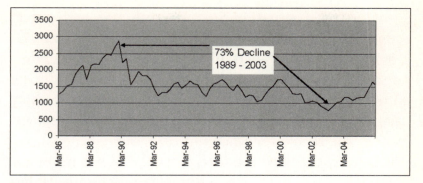

Figure 3.3   Japan Stock Market

sentiment was that Prime Minister Junichiro Koizumi finally showed the political will to take on the entrenched Japanese bureaucracy. One of the prevailing themes of modern Japan has been the power of the bureaucracy and the stability of the political system. Many of the same people and same faces have been in political power for most of the last 40 years. Prime Minister Koizumi's moves to proceed with a revamp of the postal bank system were significant, but their importance to investors was not so much in what was actually being done but that anything was being done at all. Koizumi threatened to resign if his position was not backed by the parliament. They blinked. Many of the stories you're reading about Japan today mention the improved consumer confidence and improved business environment as a result of the strength that was shown by the government to do what needed to be done—even though it was difficult and, in some quarters, unpopular.

Here is a situation in which the second-largest economy in the world seems to be undergoing a fundamental shift. After years of weak performance, underperformance, and recession, the Japanese economy finally appears to be on more solid footing. So how do we play this trend? What stocks can we buy to help us profit from a true recovery in Japan?

Let's go back to the Internet, this time using www .ADR.com, a web site run by JPMorgan. The site allows you to search the ADR universe by industry, region, or country. Searching for Japan, you find that there are 157 ADRs from Japanese companies, which range from machinery and banking companies to Internet and real estate companies. Let's find a basket of stocks that allows us to play a trend of recovery in Japan. For this exercise, we'll choose one industrial company, one bank, and one technology company.

There are 12 ADRs from Japanese banks that trade in the United States. First, let's take a look at the banking giant Mitsubishi UFJ. This is a $120 billion market capitalization conglomerate. The shares trade at a price/earnings (P/E) ratio of 16 times trailing earnings. "Trailing," in this case, means looking at what has already been reported by the company from its performance over the past 12 months. It's not an ideal measure because stock prices typically focus on the future, but we can use it in an environment where there might not be projections or future estimated earnings and we can use it to compare companies within the same sector. The shares also trade at 2.1 times price-to-book value and are up a very dramatic 59 percent over the past eight months. Although I accept that an improvement in the Japanese economy is certain to benefit the banks, I have a hard time buying into a company that is already up so much in the year to date. Let's look for something that hasn't been quite as strong. See Exhibit 3.5.

Bank of Fukuoka is a regional full-service bank in the Fukuoka Prefecture, which currently trades at a P/E of 19 times. While this is a little bit more expensive than Mitsubishi USJ, the shares are only up 20 percent year to date. I don't want to buy a stock just because it has underperformed (often stocks underperform for a reason). The year-to-date 20 percent rise is respectable but not over the top, and I fear that investors are using Mitsubishi UFJ as a play on the Japanese economy because of its size and liquidity. Bank of Fukuoka is a $5 billion company that is profitable and appears to be reasonably valued. A number of the other banks also appear to be good investments, and any one of them should be considered a viable play on growth in the Japanese economy. See Exhibit 3.6.

Among the industrial companies, let's take a look at Kawasaki Heavy Industries. This company manufactures heavy equipment and transportation equipment in addition to its well-known motorcycle brands and shipbuilding ventures. It also has a respectable business in the gas turbine industry. The share trades at a P/E of 39 times and a price-to-book of 2.3. The shares were up by

Mitsubishi UFJ Financial Group Inc

Country: Japan	Sector: Banking		
US Ticker	Price as of 02/21/06	52-week range:	Dividend:	Yield:
MTU	$13.60	$14.45-$8.1	$0.05	0.4%

COMPANY DESCRIPTION

Mitsubishi Tokyo Financial Group, Inc. operates as the holding company for The Bank of Tokyo-Mitsubishi, Ltd. (BTM) and The Mitsubishi Trust and Banking Corporation (MTB). BTM, a Japanese commercial banking organization, provides a range of domestic and international banking services in Japan and worldwide. As of June 1, 2005, its network in Japan included 251 branches, 28 sub-branches, 60 loan plazas, 474 branch automated teller machines (ATMs), and 19,062 convenience store-based, non-exclusive ATMs. The bank offers retail banking, commercial banking, global corporate banking, investment banking and asset management, operations services, treasury; and other services to individual customers in Japan through its branch offices and other direct distribution channels, as well as to large corporations, and to medium-sized and small businesses. MTU is one of the largest banking groups in Japan.

SALES AND EARNINGS (in millions, except per-share data)								KEY RATIOS (%)			
FY ends	Sales	EBIT	Pre-Tax Profit	Net Profit	EPS	CF/S	Div.	Sales Growth	EBITDA Margin	Pre-tax Margin	ROE
3/08E	5,608	1,620	1,898	n/a	n/a	n/a	0.00	6.3%	28.9%	33.8%	n/a
3/07E	5,278	1,685	1,548	n/a	0.63	n/a	0.00	5.1%	31.9%	29.3%	n/a
3/06E	5,023	1,533	1,555	n/a	0.78	n/a	0.00	106.1%	30.5%	31.0%	9.4%
3/05A	2,437	n/a	721	416.1	0.47	n/a	0.00	-10.7%	n/a	29.6%	21.4%
3/04A	2,728	n/a	1,180	822.8	0.67	n/a	0.00	n/a	n/a	43.3%	8.0%

Average Growth Rates:

	Sales	EBIT	Pre-Tax Profit	Net Profit	EPS
06-08E	6%	3%	10%	n/a	n/a
04-05A	-11%	n/a	-39%	-49%	n/a

VALUATION

P/E 3/07E	21.6x	Price/Book	2.1x
P/E 3/06E	17.4x	EV/Mkt Cap	1.4x
CFLO/Revs 3/05	0.2x	P/CFLO per share	n/a

BALANCE SHEET SUMMARY (as of 3/31/05)

Current assets	165	Current Liabilities	809
Fixed assets	5	Long-term debt	134
Other assets	837	Other liabilities	63
		Equity	41
Total assets	1,007	Total liab.s & equity	1,007
		L-T Debt/Capital	n/a

SHARE DATA

Market cap (US$ mil.)	138,702	Avg. Daily Vol. (000)	1.08
Primary shares (mil.)	6.6	Avg. Daily Vol. ($ mn) $	14.0
Float (mil.)	n/a	Institutional ownership	2.3%
		Insider ownership	0.0%

RIEDEL RESEARCH GROUP INC OBJECTIVE EQUITY RESEARCH

Exhibit 3.5 Mitsubishi UFJ
(Riedel Research Group, data from Reuters)

Bank of Fukuoka

Country: Japan	Sector: Banking		
US Ticker	Price as of 02/21/0 6	52-week range:	Dividend:	Yield:
BFKAY.PK	$76.60	$88.6 - 55.7	$0.67	0.9%

COMPANY DESCRIPTION

Largest regional bank in Kyushu, and upper-ranking regional bank. Engaged in telephone banking thru terminals, and largest scale among regional banks. Ranks 5th in terms of fund volume. Pulled out of oversease business. Noted for solid financial base. Re-focusing on retail banking within Fukuoka Pref.

		SALES AND EARNINGS (in millions, except per-share data)						KEY RATIOS (%)			
FY ends:	Sales	Operating Profit	Pre-Tax Profit	Net Profit	EPS	CF/S	Div.	Sales Growth	EBITDA Margin	Pre-ta x Margin	ROE
3/08E	164,131	77,519	71,530	38,719	57.40	n/a	n/a	3.8%	47.2%	43.6%	n/a
3/07E	158,171	67,330	57,690	34,050	49.83	n/a	n/a	-0.2%	42.6%	36.5%	n/a
3/06A	158,425	60,877	53,700	32,225	57.40	n/a	4.50	-4.4%	38.4%	33.9%	n/a
3/05A	165,639	n/a	44,716	25,949	n/a	n/a	2.50	2.4%	n/a	27.0%	7.3%
3/04A	161,785	n/a	42,297	19,956	n/a	n/a	2.50	n/a	n/a	26.1%	5.9%

Average Growth Rates:

06-08E	2%	13%	15%	10%	0%
04-05A	2%	n/a	6%	30%	n/a

VALUATION

P/E 3/08E	13.2x	Price/Book	1.5x
P/E 3/07E	15.3x	FV/EBITDA 3/07E	9.6
CFLO/Sales	3.31x	P/CFLO per share	12x

BALANCE SHEET SUMMARY (as of 3/31/05)

Current assets		Current Liabilities	
Fixed assets	136	Long-term debt	
Other assets	7,213	Other liabilities	6,979
		Equity	368
Total assets	7,349	Total liab.s & equity	7,349
		L-T Debt/Capital	n/a

SHARE DATA

Market cap (US$ mil.)	5,182	Avg. Daily Vol. (000)	5,800
Primary shares (mil.)	677.0	Avg. Daily Vol. ($ mn)	$ 441
Float (mil.)	n/a	Institutional ownership	21.0%
		Insider ownership	13.0%

RIEDEL
RESEARCH GROUP INC OBJECTIVE EQUITY RESEARCH

Source: Riedel Research Group; Reuters

Exhibit 3.6 Bank of Fukuoka
(Riedel Research Group, data from Reuters)

69 percent in 2005. Let's look for another play. Mitsubishi Electric makes and sells electrical machinery including everything from satellites to washing machines. The shares are up a respectable 29 percent year to date and traded a respectable but not overwhelming 1.2 times price-to-book. The P/E also looks high at 38 times, but a quick glance at future estimates indicates that the company is expected to grow very, very quickly in the next couple of years. Given the diversified nature of the company's business, a reasonable pace of year-to-date stock price appreciation, and the prospect of solid earnings growth, let's use Mitsubishi as a way to play the industrial sector in Japan. See Exhibit 3.7.

You can get a little bit more creative in the technology sector by looking at something connected to telephone systems and services or at computer or software companies. In the office equipment space, take a look at Ricoh or perhaps NEC. Ricoh makes a well-known line of copiers, printers, fax machines, and scanners. Ricoh shares, however, are down 14 percent year to date. Given the strength we have seen in the Japanese banks and industrial sector, there seems to be some concern in the market about either Ricoh's particular product lines or perhaps competition in some of the businesses where the company participates. I think the market is telling us enough here with the way the shares have performed that we should move on. It's not that I don't like stocks that are underperforming, but a stock that's negative when it seems the rest of the market has been very positive might be more work to understand and more risk than it's worth. Brother and NEC seem to have the same problem—both of those stocks are down year to date as well. Clearly something is going on in the office equipment sector, and the markets are telling us that they don't like it. See Exhibit 3.8.

What about in the telecom sector? The largest Japanese telecom company is Nippon Telegraph and Telephone (NTT). This is a $49 billion company that trades at a P/E of 11 times, and the shares are up 5 percent year to date. The company has 50 percent market share in mobile phones and long-distance calls in Japan and has been expanding internationally in recent years. As Chapter 6 discusses, I don't usually like to buy into regulatory systems. I don't think that a market that is protected because of a government rule and a company that benefits from that protection are usually very good investments, but clearly the telephone business in Japan is wide open and very competitive. It's a business that benefits from growing wealth and wages as people spend more on services, mobile phones, and so on. It also benefits from growing business activity, as businesses that are expanding hire more people, add more lines, and use more telephone service, all of which contribute to NTT's revenue. I would want to spend time reading recent news reports and items about NTT just to be sure that the business is solid, but telephone services are a good play on a growing economy, the price seems reasonable, and the opportunities are clearly there. Let's use NTT as our technology play on the Japanese recovery. See Exhibit 3.9.

Kawasaki Heavy Industries

Country: Japan	Sector: Manufacturing		
US Ticker	Price as of 02/21/06	52-week range:	Dividend:	Yield:
KWHIY.PK	$13.10	$16.2 - $6.6	$0.08	0.6%

COMPANY DESCRIPTION

Comprehensive heavy electric machinery and engineering company showing its strength in three fields of land, sea, and air. Also major shipbuilder and prominent motorcycle manufacturer. Highly competitive in railway rollingstock and medium-size gas turbines. Management focused on "quality followed by quantity."

SALES AND EARNINGS (in millions, except per-share data)								KEY RATIOS (%)			
FY ends:	Sales	EBITDA	Pre-Tax Profit	Net Profit	EPS	CF/S	Div.	Sales Growth	EBITDA Margin	Pre-tax Margin	ROE
12/08E	1,320,983	85,950	n/a	29,000	19.5	44.0	0.00	1.9%	6.5%	n/a	n/a
12/07E	1,296,086	80,550	n/a	24,300	16.5	40.2	0.00	0.1%	6.2%	n/a	n/a
12/06A	1,295,238	64,850	n/a	15,425	10.5	32.4	0.00	4.3%	5.0%	n/a	n/a
12/05A	1,241,591	n/a	20,564	12,069	7.9	n/a	2.40	7.0%	n/a	1.7%	5.7%
12/04A	1,160,252	n/a	11,241	6,526	n/a	n/a	2.00	n/a	n/a	1.0%	3.3%

Average Growth Rates:

	Sales	EBITDA	Pre-Tax Profit	Net Profit	EPS
06-08E	1%	15%	n/a	37%	37%
04-05A	7%	n/a	83%	85%	n/a

VALUATION

P/E 12/08E	2.9x	Price/Book	20.2x
P/E 12/07E	16.2	FV/EBITDA 12/07E	11.6x
Price/Revs 12/07E	0.06	P/CFLO per share	n/a

BALANCE SHEET SUMMARY (as of 6/30/05)

Current assets	837,004	Current Liabilities	698,482
Fixed assets	357,467	Long-term debt	207,278
Other assets	0	Other liabilities	87,248
		Equity	201,464
Total assets	1,194,472	Total liab.s & equity	1,194,472
		L-T Debt/Capital	17.4%

SHARE DATA

Market cap (US$ mil.)	5,093	Avg. Daily Vol. (mn)	2,464
Primary shares (mil.)	1,483.8	Avg. Daily Vol. ($ mn)	$ 0.32
Float (mil.)	n/a	Institutional ownership	8.0%
		Insider ownership	24.0%

Exhibit 3.7 Kawasaki Heavy Industries
(Riedel Research Group, data from Reuters)

63

Ricoh

Country: Japan　　　　Sector: Manufacturing

US Ticker	Price as of 2/21/06	52-week range:	Dividend:	Yield:
RICOY.OB	$92.85	$100-$73	$0.99	1.1%

COMPANY DESCRIPTION

Comprehensive manufacturer of Office Automation equipment. Top-ranked among domestic makers of copiers and fax machines. Produces copiers in US, UK, France and China, and fax machines in S. Korea and China. Aggressive toward tie-ups with major overseas firms. Strengthening overseas sales network thru M&A strategy.

SALES AND EARNINGS (in millions, except per-share data)

FY ends:	Sales	EBITDA	Pre-tax Profit	Net Profit	EPS	CF/S	Div.	Sales Growth	EBITDA Margin	Pre-tax Margin	ROE
12/07E	66,958,942	8,840,347	8,937,917	n/a	1,558.2	1,863.3	501.6	9.1%	13.2%	13.3%	n/a
12/06E	61,349,769	8,091,211	8,374,053	n/a	1,379.0	1,532.3	440.4	2.4%	13.2%	13.6%	n/a
12/05E	59,932,900	7,860,098	8,415,437	n/a	1,382.7	1,672.1	386.9	35.2%	13.1%	14.0%	9.6%
12/04A	44,344,572	n/a	8,007,203	6,381,839	n/a	n/a		40.7%	n/a	18.1%	11.5%
12/03A	31,512,954	n/a	7,039,250	5,147,682	n/a	n/a		n/a	n/a	22.3%	11.3%

Average Growth Rates:

	Sales	EBITDA	Pre-tax Profit	Net Profit	EPS
06-07E	6%	6%	3%	n/a	6%
03-04A	41%	n/a	14%	24%	n/a

VALUATION

P/E 12/07E	35.8x	Price/Book	1.8x
P/E 12/06E	40.4x	FV/EBITDA 12/06E	8.8
Price/Revs 12/06E	0.8x	P/CFLO per share	0.517

SHARE DATA

Market cap (US$ mil.)	13,481	Avg. Daily Vol. (000)	25,511
Primary shares (mil.)	146.8	Avg. Daily Vol. ($ mn)	$ 2.4
Float (mil.)	n/a	Institutional ownership	17.0%
		Insider ownership	16.0%

BALANCE SHEET SUMMARY (as of 6/30/05)

Current assets	1,029,747	Current Liabilities	671,514
Fixed assets	923,992	Long-term debt	226,567
Other assets	0	Other liabilities	192,590
		Equity	862,998
Total assets	1,953,669	Total liab.s & equity	1,953,669
		L-T Debt/Capital	11.6%

KEY RATIOS (%)

RIEDEL

RESEARCH GROUP INC OBJECTIVE EQUITY RESEARCH

Exhibit 3.8 Ricoh
(Riedel Research Group, data from Reuters)

NIPPON TELEGRAPH AND TELEPHONE CORP

Country: Japan			
	Sector: Telecommunications		

US Ticker	Price as of 02/21/06	52-week range:	Dividend:	Yield:
NTT	$21.83	$25.84-20.08	$0.25	1.1%

COMPANY DESCRIPTION

Nippon Telegraph and Telephone Corporation (NTT) provides fixed and mobile voice-related services, Internet Protocol/packet communications services, sales of telecommunications equipment, systems integration, and other telecommunications related services in Japan. It primarily provides regional communications, long distance and international communications, mobile communications, and data communications services in Japan. The principal services in the regional, and long distance and international communications business include intraprefectural communications services, international communications services, and related ancillary services. The principal services in the mobile communications business include cellular services, personal handyphone system services, Quickcast services, and related ancillary services. The company's data communications business includes systems integration and network systems services. Its other services include building maintenance, real property leasing, systems development, leasing, and research and development. NTT was formed in 1952 and is headquartered in Tokyo, Japan.

66

SALES AND EARNINGS (in millions, except per-share data)							KEY RATIOS (%)			
ends:	Sales	Operating Profit	Pre-Tax Profit	Net Profit	EPS	CF/S	Div.	Sales Growth	Operating Margin	Pre-tax Margin	ROE
12/08E	89,342	n/a	n/a	n/a	1.77	n/a	n/a	-0.7%	n/a	n/a	n/a
12/07E	89,966	n/a	n/a	n/a	1.69	n/a	n/a	-0.2%	n/a	n/a	n/a
12/06E	90,161	n/a	n/a	n/a	1.55	n/a	n/a	-16.6%	n/a	n/a	n/a
12/05A	108,059	n/a	1,723	1,009.4	n/a	n/a	0.13	-2.6%	n/a	1.6%	10.5%
12/04A	110,955	n/a	1,527	924.1	n/a	n/a	0.08	n/a	n/a	1.4%	10.1%

Average Growth Rates:

	Sales	Operating Profit	Pre-Tax Profit	Net Profit	EPS
06-08E	0%	n/a	n/a	n/a	7%
03-05A	-3%	n/a	13%	9%	n/a

VALUATION

P/E 12/08E	14.8x	Price/Book	0.5x
P/E 12/07E	15.5x	FV/EBITDA 12/07E	3.3
Price/Revs 12/07E	0.33x	P/CFLO per share	120.61

SHARE DATA

Market cap (US$ mil.)	44,959	Avg. Daily Vol. (000)	0.35m
Primary shares (mil.)	2,988.0	Avg. Daily Vol. (US$)	$ 8
Float (mil.)	n/a	Institutional ownership	2.0%
		Insider ownership	0.0%

BALANCE SHEET SUMMARY (as of 6/30/05)

Current assets	4,516,613	Current Liabilities	3,679,579
Fixed assets	14,581,971	Long-term debt	4,511,596
Other assets	0	Other liabilities	4,138,806
		Equity	6,768,603
Total assets	19,098,584	Total liab.s & equity	19,098,584
		L-T Debt/Capital	23.6%

RIEDEL

RESEARCH GROUP INC OBJECTIVE EQUITY RESEARCH

Exhibit 3.9 Nippon Telegraph and Telephone
(Riedel Research Group, data from Reuters)

So we have a bank that gives us exposure to business services in a growing corporate environment. It's not the largest of the banks, but it seems to be reasonably valued. We have Mitsubishi for a play on the industrial sector and a recovery in Japanese business activity. And finally, we have NTT on the telecommunications side, providing both mobile and regular telephone service in addition to broadband connections and other things related to growing affluence, disposable income, and business activity.

Note that by focusing on different sectors and quite different companies, we've lowered our risk but stayed true to the theme of buying based on Japanese business growth and economic recovery. It would be highly unlikely that our bank stock would go down because of something that happened in the industrial sector, or vice versa. Likewise, the fortunes of the telephone company are not tied to Mitsubishi's performance. All three of the stocks are run to benefit (or be hurt) according to the unique performance of their particular businesses as well as the Japanese economy and business environment as a whole. That's the theme we want to play.

Theme 3: Latin America Enters a Period of Sustained Growth Driven by Exports

Latin America is a sorely underappreciated continent. Of course, there many people who are fans of Brazilian beef, Argentine tango, and Chilean wine, but all the business community can remember is the debt defaults of the 1970s and 1980s.

The debt defaults were tragic, but they're well behind us now, and a new generation of politicians is taking over in Latin America. From a business and investing point of view, some of these politicians are good and some of them not so good. You'd be hard-pressed to find a businessperson who is a fan of Hugo Chávez in Venezuela. His populist actions and his even more extreme rhetoric have made businesspeople and investors rightfully nervous. Venezuela is a major oil exporter providing Chávez with the funds to do what he wants and, unfortunately, the arrogance to say what he wants.

On the other end of the spectrum, however, are the things that are happening in Chile, Argentina, and Brazil. Chile has been held up as a great example of the privatization of the pension program. Without going into the details of this, suffice it to say that a large bureaucracy was ended and a considerable economic force unleashed in Chile.

In Brazil, the moves have been even more impressive. The government of President Luiz Inácio Lula da Silva still faces many of the corruption issues and other challenges of previous administrations, but its economic policies have been very business friendly and welcoming to investors. As the fifth-largest country in the world in terms of population, Brazil is too big to ignore. The Brazilian economy has $1.5 trillion in purchasing power parity, making it one of the most significant players on the global stage. The country is a major exporter of agricultural products such as coffee, soybeans, wheat, rice, corn, and sugarcane. In certain commodities (soybeans, for example), Brazil is a major player. Other exportable commodities, including iron ore, contribute badly needed income and export opportunities to the Brazilian economy. This is especially noteworthy when seen in the light of China's seemingly insatiable appetite for these commodities. An economy the size of China's growing as quickly as it is demands tremendous inputs.

So let's find some ways to play this growth. We can consider various themes when thinking about Brazil. We can think about the theme of Brazil as an exporter to growing economies like China or we can consider the impact of that trade on Brazil itself. What I mean is that as the company exports products, money flows into the economy. That money will be used to buy products and services and is certainly going to impact the banking system.

With regard to Brazil as a trade play, we can think about companies that benefit from trade overall as well as companies that produce the particular commodities and products that Brazil is exporting.

One interesting company that provides exposure to Brazil as a trading powerhouse is All America Latina Logistica SA. This $1.7 billion market company is a leading provider of logistics to Brazilian exporters and can be considered a good play on increased export activity out of Brazil. See Exhibit 3.10.

One of Brazil's largest companies, Companhia Vale do Rio Doce (CVRD) is the fourth-largest global diversified mining company by market cap, as well as the world's largest producer and exporter of iron ore and pellets and one of the leading providers of manganese and ferroalloys. The company also has operations in copper, oxide, potash, alumina, aluminum, and so on. This is a huge mining company. Interestingly, the company is also the largest logistics service provider in Brazil as a result of the fact that it owns and operates railways and ports. So with CVRD you are getting a double play: both the products that are being exported and the process of exporting. Demand for the company's commodities has been huge. Global growth has been very strong, especially in resource-hungry countries like China and India.

CVRD is a $15 billion market company with adequate liquidity that trades at a P/E ratio of 12.4 times. My one concern about CVRD is that the stock is currently up nearly 50 percent year to date, and that's on top of a 50 percent gain last year and a 100 percent gain the year before. However, given the strong growth in all of the items that see CVRD mines and exports and given all the news that I've read about strong demand and pricing for commodities, the price gain is probably justified. The P/E appears quite reasonable at just 12 times, especially considering the strong growth that people are

All America Latina Logistica SA

Country: Brazil	Sector: Transportation		
US Ticker	Price as of 02/21/06	52-week range:	Dividend:	Yield:
ALLL4.SA	$22.51	25.4-11.4	$0.60	2.7%

COMPANY DESCRIPTION

The Group's principal activities are cargo transport, warehousing, storage, logistics and investments in other companies involved in similar activities. It operates its activities through rail, road and port channels. The Group also has interests to acquire, lease or lend locomotives, wagons and other rail equipment for third party.

Note: Chart shows local listing in Brazil

72

	SALES AND EARNINGS (in millions, except per-share data)							KEY RATIOS (%)			
FY ends:	Sales	EBITDA	Pre-tax Profit	Net Profit	EPS	CF/S	Div.	Sales Growth	EBITDA Margin	Pre-tax Margin	ROE
12/07E	1,494.2	606	n/a	n/a	5.00	2.25	0.25	16.2%	n/a	n/a	n/a
12/06E	1,285.5	506	n/a	n/a	4.00	1.79	0.67	17.5%	n/a	n/a	n/a
12/05E	1,093.7	431	65	n/a	2.66	0.73	0.60	15.4%	n/a	n/a	n/a
12/04A	947.7	n/a	135	150.6	n/a	n/a	0.00	24.7%	n/a	14.2%	21.0%
12/03A	760	n/a	4.0	10.2	n/a	n/a	0.00	n/a	n/a	0.5%	3.0%

Average Growth Rates:

	Sales	EBITDA	Pre-tax Profit	Net Profit	EPS	CF/S
05-07E	17%	19%	n/a	n/a	37%	76%
03-04A	25%	n/a	3304%	1384%	n/a	n/a

VALUATION

P/E 12/07E	4.4x	Price/Book	4.5x
P/E 12/06E	1.3x	EV/Total Mkt Cap	5.6x
Price/Revs 12/06E	n/a	P/CFLO per share	3.4x

BALANCE SHEET SUMMARY (as of 6/30/05)

Current assets	973	Current Liabilities	512
Fixed assets	1,176	Long-term debt	802
Other assets	0	Other liabilities	97
		Equity	739
Total assets	2,149	Total liab.s & equity	2,149
		L-T Debt/Capital	108.5%

SHARE DATA

Market cap (US$ mil.)	5,423	Avg. Daily Vol. (000)	6.58
Primary shares (mil.)	144.6	Avg. Daily Vol. ($ 000)	$ 138.2
Float (mil.)	n/a	Institutional ownership	2.0%
		Insider ownership	39.0%

RIEDEL
RESEARCH GROUP INC OBJECTIVE EQUITY RESEARCH

Exhibit 3.10 All America Latina Logística
(Riedel Research Group, data from Reuters.)

73

expecting in all these commodities. This is a situation where the year-to-date growth in the stock might be justified, and at this reasonable valuation, I am willing to take that risk. See Exhibit 3.11.

The telecom market in Brazil provides a wide variety of investment options. All of these companies benefit from the second level of impact of the exporting. They're clearly not exporting telecom services, but the rising affluence, disposable income, and business activity will drive telecom activity. This is similar to our discussion of NTT in Japan being a play on growing business activity there. We might want to use Brasil Telecom or one of the cellular providers as a way to play growth in Brazil. My personal preference is for the fixed-line companies, typically the larger companies. Something that is well financed and well positioned. Let's take a look at Brasil Telecom.

Brasil Telecom is a $3 billion company that trades in New York under the ticker BRP. A quick look at the Yahoo!Finance web site shows that the shares trade at 12 times the outlook for EPS (earnings per share) for 2006. Comparing that P/E to the company's expected growth rate, we see that the PEG ratio (price–to–earnings growth) is 0.5 times. This means that the company is trading at a P/E that is about half of its expected growth rate. Let's think about this. We have a company that is trading at 12 times and analysts are telling us they expect it to grow at 25 percent on average during the next five years. Imagine what you would have to pay for a 25 percent growth stock in the United States—20 times? 30 times?

But there are some issues here. Over the past couple of years there has been a dispute among some major shareholders. Recent news indicates that that issue is being settled. We also see from the Yahoo! headlines that the company was not profitable in the most recent quarter. A quick read of the article, however, reveals that a series of unusual, or one-time, charges hurt profits in the most recent quarter and that the expectation is that the company will be profitable in the near term. The company is seeing great growth in its cellular business and in its broadband connections. This is one of the significant advantages that large-scale fixed-line telephone companies have in developing economies. They are often the first ones to be rolling out broadband connections, which in most situations (especially where there is economic growth) are taken up much faster than was anticipated. The demand for Internet connections in the modern world is tremendously strong and the adoption in the developing countries can be much faster than people might expect. Telephone companies are a great way to play this trend. See Exhibit 3.12.

You might also want to take a look at Brazilian cellular provider TIM Participacoes (TSU). As you'll see, many analysts are enthusiastic about this company and, while the shares have been strong so far this year, the expectation is for continued growth.

As Chapter 8 discusses, banks are one way to play

Companhia Vale do Rio Doce

Country: Brazil	Sector: Mining

US Ticker	Price as of 02/21/06	52-week range:	Dividend:	Yield:
RIO	$45.86	$51.27-25.6	$1.39	3.0%

COMPANY DESCRIPTION

Valley of the Rio Doce Company engages primarily in mining and logistics businesses. It engages in iron ore mining, pellet production, manganese ore mining, and ferroalloy production, as well as in the production of nonferrous minerals, such as kaolin, potash, copper, and gold. The company's aluminum-related operations include bauxite mining, alumina refining, and aluminum metal smelting. Valley of the Rio Doce holds exploration claims that cover 12.0 million hectares in Brazil; and 3.8 million hectares in Gabon, Chile, Mozambique, Mongolia, Argentina, and Peru. In addition, it operates logistics systems, such as railroads and ports that are integrated with its mining operations. Further, the company has interests in nine hydroelectric power generation projects and three steel companies. Valley of the Rio Doce was founded in 1942 and is headquartered in Rio De Janeiro, Brazil.

	SALES AND EARNINGS (in millions, except per-share data)							KEY RATIOS (%)			
			Pre-Tax	Net				Sales	EBITDA	Pre-tax	
FY ends:	Sales	EBITDA	Profit	Profit	EPS	CF/S	Div.	Growth	Margin	Margin	ROE
12/07E	17,392	n/a	n/a	n/a	5.77	n/a	n/a	9.6%	n/a	n/a	n/a
12/06E	15,868	n/a	n/a	n/a	5.41	n/a	n/a	24.1%	n/a	n/a	n/a
12/05E	12,791	n/a	n/a	n/a	4.17	n/a	n/a	-53.6%	n/a	n/a	46.7%
12/04A	27,544	n/a	9,013	7,203.1	n/a	n/a	0.24	41.7%	n/a	32.7%	35.5%
12/03A	19,442	n/a	5,660	4,761.8	n/a	n/a	0.22	n/a	n/a	29.1%	30.2%

Average Growth Rates:

	Sales	EBITDA	Pre-Tax Profit	Net Profit	EPS	CF/S
05-07E	17%	n/a	n/a	n/a	18%	n/a
03-04A	42%	n/a	59%	51%	n/a	n/a

VALUATION

P/E 12/07E	7.9x	Price/Book	4.1x
P/E 12/06E	8.5x	EV/Total Mkt Cap	1.1x
Price/Revs 12/06E	2.7x	P/CFLO per share	n/a

BALANCE SHEET SUMMARY (as of 6/30/05)

Current assets	11,930	Current Liabilities	9,327
Fixed assets	31,542	Long-term debt	9,045
Other assets	0	Other liabilities	6,932
		Equity	18,169
Total assets	43,472	Total liab.s & equity	43,472
		L-T Debt/Capital	20.8%

SHARE DATA

Market cap (US$ mil.)	50,986	Avg. Daily Vol. (000)	3,003
Primary shares (mil.)	735.8	Avg. Daily Vol. ($ mn)	$ 135
Float (mil.)	n/a	Institutional ownership	16.0%
		Insider ownership	n/a

RIEDEL

RESEARCH GROUP INC OBJECTIVE EQUITY RESEARCH

Exhibit 3.11 Companhia Vale do Rio Doce (CVRD) (Riedel Research Group, data from Reuters)

Brasil Telecom Participacoes SA

Country: Brazil		Sector: Telecommunication	
US Ticker	Price as of 02/21/06	52-week range:	Dividend:	Yield:
BRP	$41.00	45.18-30.69	$1.94	4.9%

COMPANY DESCRIPTION

*Brazil Telecom provides local and long-distance telecom services
in Brazil. The company offers various services that include local
services, such as calls that originate and terminate within a single
local area in the region, as well as installation, monthly
subscription, measured services, public telephones, and
supplemental local services; intraregional long-distance services,
which include intrastate and interstate; interregional and
international long-distance services; network services, including
interconnection, leasing of facilities that include leasing trunk lines
to cellular service providers for use within their own network, and
fixed-to-mobile services; data transmission services; wireless
mobile services; and other services. In addition, it provides a
range value-added services, such as call forwarding, voice mail,
caller ID, call waiting, and directory inquiry voice service, as well
as advertising on public telephone cards. The company was
founded in 1998 and is based in Brasilia, Brazil.*

SALES AND EARNINGS (in millions, except per-share data)								KEY RATIOS (%)			
FY ends:	Sales	EBITDA	Pre-Tax Profit	Net Profit	EPS	CF/S	Div.	Sales Growth	EBITDA Margin	Pre-ta x Margin	ROE
12/07E	12,211	4,496	1,684	2,192	31.62	31.54	n/a	4.4%	36.8%	13.8%	26.1%
12/06E	11,691	3,686	462	601	22.56	14.97	n/a	13.6%	31.5%	4.0%	9.7%
12/05A	10,294	3,209	(299)	(313)	19.64	7.23	2.13	13.6%	31.2%	-2.9%	1.3%
12/04A	9,065	3,565	202	-79.4	18.11	3.78	1.44	14.5%	39.3%	2.2%	6.1%
12/03A	7,915	3,304 #	(41) #	-34.7	n/a	5.11	n/a	n/a	41.7%	-0.5%	4.4%

Average Growth Rates:

	Sales	EBITDA	Pre-Tax Profit	Net Profit	EPS	CF/S
05-07E	9%	18%	n/a	n/a	27%	109%
03-04A	15%	8%	n/a	n/a	n/a	-26%

VALUATION

P/E 12/07E	1.3x	Price/Book	0.4x
P/E 12/06E	1.8x	FV/EBITDA 12/06E	2.4
Price/Revs 12/06E	0.3x	P/CFLO per share	5.7

BALANCE SHEET SUMMARY (as of 6/30/05)

Current assets	6,742	Current Liabilities	4,613
Fixed assets	11,980	Long-term debt	3,852
Other assets	0	Other liabilities	4,128
		Equity	6,128
Total assets	18,722	Total liab.s & equity	18,722
		L-T Debt/Capital	20.6%

SHARE DATA

Market cap (US$ mil.)	3,364	Avg. Daily Vol. (000)	0.33
Primary shares (mil.)	26.5	Avg. Daily Vol. ($ mm)	$ 13.53
Float (mil.)	n/a	Institutional ownership	35.0%
		Insider ownership	0.0%

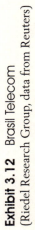

RIEDEL

RESEARCH GROUP INC OBJECTIVE EQUITY RESEARCH

Exhibit 3.12 Brasil Telecom
(Riedel Research Group, data from Reuters)

Banco Itau Holding Financeira SA

Country: Brazil		Sector: Banking	
US Ticker	Price as of 02/21/06	52-week range:	Dividend:	Yield:
ITU	$31.80	$30.8-$15.49	$0.14	0.0%

COMPANY DESCRIPTION

Banco Itau Holding Financeira S.A. offers banking services to individuals and corporations in Brazil and internationally. It provides a range of retail banking services, asset management and capitalization plans for individuals and very small businesses, as well as provides personalized services to high-income individuals. The bank offers financial advisory services, financial consulting services, and a range of traditional banking and insurance products. Banco Itau also provides various financial products and services to middle market customers. In addition, it offers portfolio management services as well as automobile, life, property, casualty, and health insurance. As of June 30, 2005, it operated a network of 2,290 branches in Brazil. The company has strategic alliance agreements with Banco BMG S.A. and America Online Latin America, Inc. Banco Itau Holding was founded in 1944 and is based in Sao Paulo, Brazil.

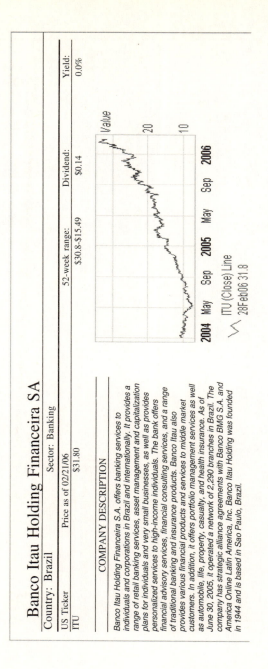

80

SALES AND EARNINGS (in millions, except per-share data)

| | | | Pre-Tax | Net | | | | KEY RATIOS (%) | | | |
FY ends:	Sales	EBITDA	Profit	Profit	EPS	CF/S	Div.	Sales Growth	EBITDA Margin	Pre-tax Margin	ROE
12/07E	n/a	n/a	n/a	n/a	2.52	n/a	n/a	n/a	n/a	n/a	n/a
12/06E	n/a	n/a	n/a	n/a	2.36	n/a	0.009	n/a	n/a	n/a	n/a
12/05A	n/a	n/a	n/a	n/a	2.04	n/a	0.004	n/a	n/a	n/a	n/a
12/04A	25,266	n/a	6,277	4,185	1.54	n/a	0.004	19.0%	n/a	24.8%	27.0%
12/03A	21,240	n/a	5,043	3,456	1.25	n/a	0.005	n/a	n/a	23.7%	26.5%

Average Growth Rates:

	Sales	EBITDA	Pre-Tax Profit	Net Profit	EPS
06-07E	n/a	n/a	n/a	n/a	7%
03-05A	n/a	n/a	n/a	n/n	n/a

VALUATION

P/E 12/07E	12.6x	Price/Book	0.6x
P/E 12/06E	13.5x	FV/EBITDA 12/06E	n/a
Price/Revs 12/04A	0.8x	P/CFLO per share	n/a

BALANCE SHEET SUMMARY (as of 6/30/05)

Current assets	-	Current Liabilities	115,174.2
Fixed assets	30,908.8	Long-term debt	-
Other assets	99,429.8	Other liabilities	1,194.4
		Equity	13,971.1
Total assets	130,338.6	Total liab.s & equity	130,338.6
		L-T Debt/Capital	n/a

SHARE DATA

Market cap (US$ mil.)	30,882	Avg. Daily Vol. (000)	1.12m
Primary shares (mil.)	137.2	Avg. Daily Vol. (US$)	$ 31
Float (mil.)	n/a	Institutional ownership	4.0%
		Insider ownership	0.0%

RIEDEL
RESEARCH GROUP INC OBJECTIVE EQUITY RESEARCH

Exhibit 3.13 Banco Itaú
(Riedel Research Group, data from Reuters)

growth in a developing economy. Brazil has had its share of banking problems, but a number of the largest companies in Brazil are the banks and thus they are a natural place to look for investment opportunities. A quick look on the JPMorgan ADR site (www.ADR.com) shows that Banco Itaú (ITU) is an $11 billion market cap company that is up 27 percent over the past 12 months and that trades at a P/E of about 12 times, half of its expected growth rate. Some of the other banks in the market have shares that are up around 100 percent year to date, including Bradesco and Unibanco. Although these might be interesting companies, with a quick look at the valuation and the fact that much of the share price appreciation has probably already taken place, I'll stick with ITU. See Exhibit 3.13.

So a bank, a mining/logistics company, and a telephone company provide us with that diversified exposure to Brazilian growth: a fairly pure play on the economic prospects for Brazil, and the opportunity to participate in this identified theme of Latin American growth.

I'm not suggesting that you should run out and buy these particular stocks. By the time this book is published, these themes will have either played out or not, and different themes will be appropriate. In this chapter, you've seen that if you have feelings about a particular trend or beliefs about particular developments around the world, you can quickly and easily find ways to play those things. You've also learned a bit about diversification. Don't just pick one theme—pick a few. Don't just pick one country, region, or industry—pick a few. But you shouldn't believe that growth in one particular region or one particular industry can be played only in that particular market. You may well find that Brazil is the cheapest way to play China or Turkey might be the cheapest way to invest in European growth.

Chapter FOUR

Understanding Relationships: Who Is Benefiting from Current Trends?

Investing in the Headlines

Without realizing it, you're walking past some of the best investment advice in the world every day. As you walk down the street you see imported cars, hybrid vehicles, new strollers, toys, kids' clothes, and people using new-fangled cellular phones. We are surrounded by investment advice and investment ideas. This chapter discusses how to translate that information into identifiable and investable ideas and themes. I encourage you to use your own experience, your friends, and the publications you read as a source of investment ideas. I happen to spend quite a lot of time reading the newspaper and getting news online. Because of my background and family history, I pay particular attention to what's happening in Europe, Australia, and Asia. But your experience may be quite different. Perhaps your work exposes you to trends in Russia or your friends introduce you to what's going on in some other region. Maybe you recently bought a car built in Korea or a computer built in Taiwan. Whatever your experience, whatever you do on a daily basis, you are always exposed to products, services, ideas, and information that you can turn into an investment idea and, hopefully, a profit.

Using the Media As a Source for Ideas

As part of my research for the writing of this book, I spent much of the past week keeping my eyes open for concepts, trends, and developments that could become investable themes. Even within the mainstream media, I was able to find a number of interesting themes. This doesn't include the more business-oriented media such as *Business Week*, *The Economist*, *Forbes*, *Fortune*, or the *Wall Street Journal*. These are themes and ideas that came straight out of the mainstream press.

Examples of Trends and Ideas

Reading today's headlines yields a wonderful array of opportunities for the international investor. Just this past week in the *New York Times*, there were headlines on the approval of the European Union (EU) draft constitution in Luxembourg, progress at the Group of Eight meetings on aid and support to Africa, pressure on the Philippines president to step down, discussion of currency revaluation in Malaysia, news of progress on a major oil refining and chemicals venture with Saudi Aramco in China, and a study of remittances to families in Mexico by workers in the United States. It is not difficult to see how any one of these stories might be part of an investment strategy.

Approval of the EU Draft Constitution in Luxembourg

One of the most interesting developments in the world over the past 20 years or so has been the substantial unification of Europe. If you think about Europe as extending from Sweden to Portugal and from France to Poland, the unification of these countries to any extent is amazing. Put in the context of wars and conflicts over the past century, any progress is astounding. Against all odds, however, unification is real. The introduction of the euro, the standardization of regulations and laws, the issuance of a common passport, and the alignment of economic and foreign policy make Europe a largely unified bloc. There are certainly still differences country by country, but the ease of doing business across this whole region has created a mostly unified market in an area that just 75 years ago was wracked by war. See Figure 4.1.

The importance of this unification for investors and businesses is difficult to overstate—a much larger market to be addressed, much larger companies to address it, and more investment opportunities. The introduction and widespread acceptance of the euro across this entire

Figure 4.1   Map of the European Union
(CIA: The World Factbook, 20 April 2006)

region at the beginning of 2002 was a very impressive achievement. Having a common currency makes transactions, business, investment, travel, and trade much simpler. The establishment of the euro could be considered one of the most impressive economic developments of the past 100 years. With business integration largely complete, the next major hurdle for the European Union is political integration. What they intend is not the elimination of state borders and state differences but the development of coordinated political goals and paths. A key feature of this effort is the constitution to be adopted by the EU. After a number of years of hammering together a draft constitution, one of the major developments of 2005 was a series of national votes on whether this draft would be acceptable.

Having suffered two dramatic defeats in France and Holland, the EU draft constitution is unlikely to get far in its current form. Subsequent approval by Luxembourg, Cyprus, and Malta might not have received the same attention as the French and Dutch defeats, but it does indicate that certain smaller countries recognize the value of the European Union and want to see progress toward a more unified Europe. Many of the countries of Eastern Europe have interesting investment opportunities that provide exposure to medium-term progress toward broader European unity. Turkey, for example, has more than 20 listed ADRs in the United States, providing exposure to banks, real estate, beverages, consumer goods, media, autos, oil and gas, and telecom. Choosing a few well-positioned Turkish companies that provide exposure to an improving economic outlook for that country as it gains more access to the European markets might prove a good medium-term opportunity. In fact, the Turkish mobile phone service provider, Turk-Cell (TKC) provided a 56 percent return in 2005 and

TurkCell

Country: Turkey		Sector: Mobile Service	
US Ticker	Price as of 2/21/06		
TKC	$19.14		

52-week range:	Dividend:	Yield:
19.60 - 12.12	$0.24	1.38%

COMPANY DESCRIPTION

Turkcell Iletisim Hizmetleri A.S. provides mobile voice and data services to subscribers throughout Turkey and neighboring states. Subscribers can choose between the Company's postpaid and prepaid services. Postpaid voice services include network access, call forwarding, call holding, call waiting, call barring, caller identification (ID) presentation and caller ID restriction, dual numbering, twin card, high-memory subscriber identification module card options, international roaming, mobile virtual private network and services, such as teleconferencing, voice mail, call alert, collect call service, unified messaging, short message service (SMS), multimedia message service, wireless application protocol-over general packet radio service, high-speed circuit switched data and circuit switched data, mobile Internet, directory service, a financial information line, fleet management, m-commerce, m-payment and mobile-marketing services. The Company also provides prepaid mobile service.

SALES AND EARNINGS (in millions, except per-share data)

FY ends:	Sales	EBITDA	Pre-Tax Profit	Net Profit	EPS	CF/S	Div.	Sales Growth	EBITDA Margin	Pre-tax Margin	ROE
12/07E	5,119	2,082	1,869	n/a	1.5	n/a	1.23	6.1%	40.7%	36.5%	n/a
12/06E	4,824	1,935	362	n/a	1.5	n/a	0.82	13.3%	40.1%	7.5%	n/a
12/05A	4,259	1,758	1,090	n/a	1.1	n/a	0.50	33.1%	41.3%	25.6%	n/a
12/04A	3,201	n/a	793	512	n/a	n/a	n/a	-9.9%	n/a	24.8%	25.8%
12/03A	3,551	n/a	543	1,116	n/a	n/a	n/a	n/a	n/a	15.3%	36.8%

KEY RATIOS (%)

Average Growth Rates:

	Sales	EBITDA	Pre-Tax Profit	Net Profit	EPS
05-07E	10%	9%	31%	n/a	16%
03-04A	-10%	n/a	46%	-54%	n/a

VALUATION

P/E 12/07E	12.4x	Price/Book	6.5x
P/E 12/06E	16.0x	FV/EBITDA 12/06E	10.2
Price/Revs 12/06E	4.1x	P/CFLO per share	n/a

SHARE DATA

Market cap (US$ mil.)	12,794	Avg. Daily Vol. (000)	0.18
Primary shares (mil.)	742.0	Avg. Daily Vol. (US$)	$ 3.45
Float (mil.)	n/a	Institutional ownership	7.0%
		Insider ownership	31.0%

BALANCE SHEET SUMMARY (as of 6/30/05)

Current assets	1,824.9	Current Liabilities	1,796.0
Fixed assets	2,536.6	Long-term debt	269.7
Other assets	0	Other liabilities	310.5
		Equity	1,985.5
Total assets	4,361.5	Total liab.s & equity	4,362
		L-T Debt/Capital	6.2%

RIEDEL
RESEARCH GROUP INC OBJECTIVE EQUITY RESEARCH

Source: Riedel Research Group; Reuters

Exhibit 4.1 TurkCell
(Riedel Research Group, data from Reuters)

appears set to move higher. U.S.-listed opportunities in Greece, Poland, Cyprus, and Hungary, as well as other countries set to benefit economically from increased integration into Europe, also provided positive returns in 2005. See Exhibit 4.1.

Progress at the Group of Eight Meetings on Aid and Support to Africa

One of the great tragedies of the second half of the twentieth century was that Africa did not experience the social and economic growth that took hold in other parts of the world. The legacy of colonialism, as well as widespread poverty and underdevelopment, unfortunately let Africa live up to its nineteenth-century moniker "the Lost Continent." We can hope that the next 100 years bring much more positive developments for this beautiful continent and its amazing inhabitants. In fact, we're starting to see a global understanding of what needs to be done.

The tremendous opportunity of Africa is clear. What is not so obvious is the steps that will be taken in the next 10 or so years to reverse the tremendous decline in the economic position of that continent. Only once the trend has reversed will there be substantial movement in investment opportunities in the countries of Africa. There are currently over 100 investment opportunities in the U.S. markets for investors looking for exposure to African companies. Many of these are South African companies, but there are also companies in Egypt, Morocco, Malawi, and Nigeria that have listings accessible to individual investors. The industries represented range from construction and fixed-line telecom to mining, media, and banks. The recent high-profile moves to increase trade and aid to Africa as well as eliminate large portions of onerous foreign debt may be the beginnings of a turnaround for Africa. Investors hoping to benefit from a longer-term improvement in the fortunes of the African continent need look no further for opportunities than their local stock exchanges.

Traditionally, many of the investment opportunities in Africa have revolved around minerals and mining. The mineral wealth of Africa is legendary and has been a target for investment and business for many decades. What is less well understood, however, is the way extraction industries lead to other pockets of economic development and growth. Of course, mined material is taken by rail to a port for export or off to another plant for processing. Every step along the way, there are workers who earn wages, businesses that provide services, and potential for investment and profit. As the mine workers, train engineers, and port operators earn and spend their wages, they produce opportunities for real estate developers, telephone companies, and so on.

A quick look on the Bank of New York ADR web site (www.bnyadr.com) shows that there are 94 ADRs from African markets. Many of these are mining companies, but there are a number of up-and-coming interesting

Johnnic Holdings Ltd

Country: South Africa   **Sector:** Communications

US Ticker	Price as of 02/21/06	52-week range:	Dividend:	Yield:
JNHLY.PK	$2.50	$4.00–$1.20	14.00	3.0%

COMPANY DESCRIPTION

Johnnic Holdings Limited is an integrated entertainment, media and telecommunication company. The Company's core holdings are Johnnic Communications Limited and MTN Group. Johnnic Communications holds investments in publishing, media and entertainment. It publishes The Sunday Times, with 3,500,000 readers each week, as well as other newspapers and magazines. It also has holdings in Gallo Music, a publisher of African music; the Exclusive Books chain of book stores, and I-Net Bridge, a supplier of electronic screen-based financial and company data and news. MTN is a telecommunication company that operates GSM (global system for mobile communication) networks in six African countries. Its networks collectively service the mobile communication needs of over 9,500,000 subscribers. The Company's non-core holdings are Gallagher Estate Holdings Limited, Johnnic Properties and Suncoast Casino. In compliance with the Black Economic Empowerment Bill, the Company is black managed.

Note: Chart Shown is for South Africa Listing of Same Company

94

SALES AND EARNINGS (in millions, except per-share data)

FY ends:	Sales	EBITDA	Pre-Tax Profit	Net Profit	EPS	CF/S	Div.
12/07E	131	30.0	20.5	149	89.00	n/a	30.00
12/06E	132	28.5	19.2	138	99.00	n/a	14.00
12/05A	151	33.9	25.1	125	62.50	n/a	150.00
12/04A	n/a	n/a	n/a	n/a	n/a	n/a	n/a
12/03A	n/a	n/a	n/a	n/a	n/a	n/a	n/a

Average Growth Rates:

	Sales	EBITDA	Pre-Tax Profit	Net Profit	EPS
05-07E	-7%	-6%	-10%	9%	19%
03-04A	n/a	n/a	n/a	n/a	n/a

VALUATION

P/E 12/07E	1.6x	Price/Book	0.2x
P/E 12/06E	n/a	FV/EBITDA 12/06E	0.2x
Price/Revs 12/06E	n/a	P/CFLO per share	n/a

SHARE DATA

Market cap (US$ mil.)	359.8	Avg. Daily Vol. (000)	277.3
Primary shares (mil.)	$ 900	Avg. Daily Vol. (US$)	104.2
Float (mil.)	54.0%	Institutional ownership	7.0%
		Insider ownership	n/a

KEY RATIOS (%)

	Sales Growth	EBITDA Margin	Pre-tax Margin	ROE
12/07E	-0.8%	22.9%	15.6%	n/a
12/06E	-12.6%	21.6%	14.5%	n/a
12/05A	n/a	22.5%	16.6%	n/a
12/04A	n/a	n/a	n/a	153.0%
12/03A	n/a	n/a	n/a	16.0%

BALANCE SHEET SUMMARY (as of 6/30/05)

Current assets	1,557	Current Liabilities	384
Fixed assets	471	Long-term debt	37
Other assets	0	Other liabilities	2
		Equity	1,605
Total assets	2,028	Total liab.s & equity	2,028
		L-T Debt/Capital	16.0%

RIEDEL
RESEARCH GROUP INC OBJECTIVE EQUITY RESEARCH

Exhibit 4.2 Johnnic
(Riedel Research Group, data from Reuters)

95

industries represented as well. Consider, for example, Bidvest Group (BVGLY). This South African investment holding company provides products and services from electrical cable to food service. Another possibility is Johnnic Communications, a very appealing South Africa–based music and media company that seems set to benefit from this increased activity and affluence across all of Africa. Remember, as well, that banks often constitute an interesting and profitable investment in regions and countries where growth is expected. There are 20 banks and finance companies among the 94 listed ADRs from Africa for a large and liquid play on African growth for the medium and long term. See Exhibit 4.2.

Pressure on the Philippine President to Step Down

The Philippines has had a long and close relationship with the United States. The fact that there are large Filipino communities in the United States, as well as many Americans with experience in the Philippines, makes the country a market that many people might consider investing in. Unfortunately, in recent years the news from the Philippines has mostly been about political unrest. You should recognize, however, that unrest often provides opportunity, and in the case of the Philippines, political unrest has presented plenty of opportunities for profit in recent years.

Investors with an interest in the Philippines might have found an intriguing opportunity in the news that pressure was mounting on the Philippines president to step down. Six of President Gloria Arroyo's ministers called for her to step down and hand power to Vice President Noli de Castro. Allegations of cheating in 2004 elections and claims that members of her family took payoffs from illegal gambling ratcheted up pressure, and this may be one of the final straws in the political upheaval in the Philippines. Since the removal of Ferdinand Marcos in 1986, popular uprisings and coups d'état have removed four Philippine administrations from power. The most recent administration to be removed as a result of concerns about corruption scandals was that of Fidel Ramos, who was pushed out of power in January 2001. His removal from office drove the local Philippine index (which had been down by 43 percent during 2000) up by 16 percent, from 1471 to 1713, in just three weeks. Investors who believe that the removal of Arroyo will reverse the anemic performance of Philippine equities have 15 depository receipts listed in the United States to provide exposure to that market. Philippine Long Distance Telephone, long a bell wether stock in that market, might provide sound liquid exposure to a recovery there. See Exhibit 4.3.

Discussion of a Currency Revaluation in Malaysia

Chapter 9 will examine currency in detail, but since it is a theme that generates a lot of ink in the newspapers, I'll mention it here as well. In considering currency,

Philippine Long Distance Telephone Co

Country: Philippines	Sector: Telecommunications		
US Ticker	Price as of 02/21/06	52-week range:	Dividend:	Yield:
PHI	$35.00	$36.00-24.25	$1.58	4.5%

COMPANY DESCRIPTION

The PLDT is the principal supplier of domestic and international telecommunications services in the Philippines. PLDT provides include digital leased lines for domestic and international communication, high-speed data transmission, high performance packet switching service and private networking.

SALES AND EARNINGS (in millions, except per-share data)

FY ends:	Sales	EBITDA	Pre-Tax Profit	Net Profit	EPS	CF/S	Div.
12/07E	2,613	n/a	n/a	n/a	3.90	n/a	n/a
12/06E	2,494	n/a	n/a	n/a	3.54	n/a	n/a
12/05A	2,365	n/a	n/a	n/a	3.26	n/a	n/a
12/04A	2,249	n/a	587	498	n/a	n/a	n/a
12/03A	1,759	n/a	207	201	n/a	n/a	n/a

KEY RATIOS (%)

	Sales Growth	EBITDA Margin	Pre-tax Margin	ROE
12/07E	4.8%	n/a	n/a	n/a
12/06E	5.5%	n/a	n/a	n/a
12/05A	n/a	n/a	n/a	n/a
12/04A	n/a	n/a	26.1%	67.0%
12/03A	n/a	n/a	11.8%	12.0%

Average Growth Rates:

	Sales	EBITDA	Pre-Tax Profit	Net Profit	EPS
05-07E	5%	n/a	n/a	n/a	9%
03-05A	28%	n/a	184%	148%	n/a

VALUATION

P/E 12/07E	7.3x	Price/Book	9.0x
P/E 12/06E	12.1x	FV/EBITDA 12/06E	11.1x
Price/Revs 12/06E	8.1x	P/CFLO per share	2.4x

SHARE DATA

Market cap (US$ mil.)	6,077	Avg. Daily Vol. (000)	0.28
Primary shares (mil.)	170.2	Avg. Daily Vol. ($ mn)	$ 10.9
Float (mil.)	n/a	Institutional ownership	18.0%
		Insider ownership	0.0%

BALANCE SHEET SUMMARY (as of 6/30/05)

Current assets	46,855	Current Liabilities	56,932
Fixed assets	218,618	Long-term debt	135,988
Other assets	0	Other liabilities	3,085
		Equity	41,702
Total assets	265,473	Total liab.s & equity	265,473
		L-T Debt/Capital	51.2%

RIEDEL RESEARCH GROUP INC OBJECTIVE EQUITY RESEARCH

Exhibit 4.3 Philippine Long Distance Telephone (Riedel Research Group, data from Reuters)

99

remember that the key question is whether the rest of the world thinks a currency is underpriced or over-priced. Money is just like any other commodity. During times of high demand, the price of it goes up; in times when no one wants to own the stuff, the price of it goes down. The influences of government policy as well as trade and global capital flows make the market slightly more complicated than the market for Coca-Cola or popcorn, but it is easy to get too worked up over the complexities of currency.

In recent years, the rising economic power of China, especially as an export engine, has led many people to be very concerned that the Chinese economy is benefiting from having a currency that is too cheap. This is possible because the government in China (as in many countries) controls the value of its currency. For many years, the Chinese yuan (or Ren Min Bi) has been pegged (or fixed) in value relative to the U.S. dollar. In the summer of 2005, this changed ever so slightly. The change, predictably, was not enough to satisfy members of the U.S. Congress, who, in their attempts to attract voters and popularity, found it convenient to point at China as a source of all our economic problems. More on that later. What I would like to discuss here is the potential opportunity in some other currencies and markets.

While revaluation of the Chinese currency gets all of the attention, there are a number of other countries globally that have benefited in recent years from exports driven by their keeping their currencies pegged to the weaker dollar. For example, the Southeast Asian country Malaysia has benefited from this trend. Malaysia's ringgit has been stable at 3.8 to the U.S. dollar since 1998, despite a dramatic recovery in the local economy from the currency crisis at that time.

By keeping its currency weak, Malaysia has benefited tremendously from an export boom that has also boosted other industries. Exports of electrical equipment, wood, palm oil, textiles, and other products have been cheaper for the world to buy because of the weak Malaysian currency. But, of course, there is no free lunch. The downside of a currency that is being held artificially high is, of course, that imported goods (including fuels and raw materials) are more expensive, which can cause inflation and dampen growth. Having a weak currency such that it takes 3.8 ringgit to buy one U.S. dollar means that products priced in U.S. dollars, such as oil, plastics, petrochemicals, and other global commodities, are expensive to bring into your country.

It's important to consider the impact of currency changes on your investments. Looking at this from the viewpoint of buying into a Malaysian company that has a listing in the United States, those investors and investments would benefit from a devaluation of the ringgit. Because the values of ADRs are in U.S. dollars and local share prices are in ringgit, a 20 percent reduction in the value of the ringgit would raise the dollar value of the ADR by 20 percent.

There are currently 13 Malaysian companies with ADRs in the U.S. market, ranging from travel companies and banks to companies that deal in electricity and food. Because the play here is not so much on Malaysia and Malaysian growth but more on the mechanics of the impact of a devaluation, it doesn't matter which of these investments you're buying. Nevertheless, be careful to buy profitable companies with reasonable valuations (more on that later) so that the risk of the stock price going down independent of the change in the currency is minimized.

Impact of Devaluation of Local Currency on ADRs

The impact of a local currency devaluation on an ADR investment is easy to see in the following example. If a stock trades in the local market at 3.8 Malaysian ringgit (equal to $1 at the current exchange rate), and an ADR represents two local shares, the ADR will be priced at U.S. $2. If the value of the ringgit falls to, say, 3 per U.S. dollar and the local share price remains at 3.8, the ADR (representing two shares of value) would now be worth $2.53. This assumes that there is no impact on the fundamentals of the business by the change in the relative value of the currencies. This simple example helps to explain why investing in ADRs, where there is a reasonable assumption that a devaluation of a local currency will take place at some point in the future, can be a significant boost to an investor's return.

Progress on a Major Oil Refining Project in China Involving ExxonMobil, Aramco, and Sinopec

The oil and gas industries have always attracted a lot of international investment. Not only are these global commodities traded widely and usually in a hard currency such as U.S. dollars, but the tremendous investment needs for exploration, development, and transportation require raising money in the capital markets. Over 100 of the ADRs traded in the United States are in oil and gas. Given the tremendous reliance on oil as the fuel of economic development, many of these have proven to be excellent investments.

When considering all the various oil and gas investment opportunities, keep your eyes open for news items such as the one I came across the other day. This news of a groundbreaking on a $3.5 billion project to triple the output of a refinery in a Fujian province provides a number of interesting investment ideas. Of course, a refinery, by definition, involves the input of crude oil and the output of a variety of refined gas products (gasoline, diesel, and so on). As a result, there are many companies that can benefit from a project of this scale to triple the output of a refinery. A quick search online reveals that investors interested in this project can invest directly in the NYSE listing of Sinopec (SHI), which will be 50 percent owner of this new venture.

There are, however, a number of potentially more interesting opportunities. Consider for a moment the

Sinopec Shanghai Petrochemical Co Ltd

Country: China	Sector: Oil and Gas		
US Ticker	Price as of 02/21/06		
SHI	$51.40		

52-week range:	Dividend:	Yield:
$51.4 - $29.83	$2.42	4.7%

COMPANY DESCRIPTION

Sinopec Shanghai Petrochemical Co. is engaged in the processing of crude oil into synthetic fibres, resins and plastics, intermediate petrochemicals and petroleum products. Through its subsidiaries, Co. is engaged in the production of resins products and polypropylene film; trading of electrical appliances; production of special sealing material; manufacturing and distribution of chemical products; trading in petrochemical products and equipment; production of vinyl acetate products; production of acrylic fibre products; and investment management.

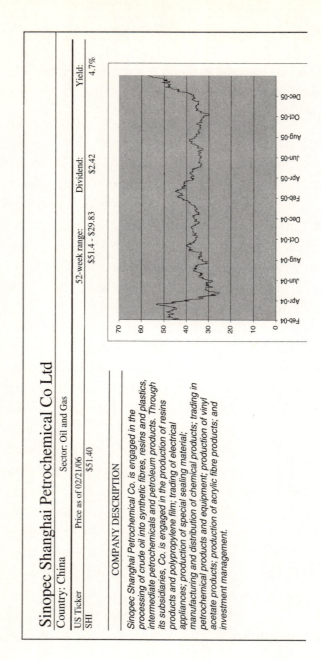

SALES AND EARNINGS (in millions, except per-share data)							KEY RATIOS (%)				
FY ends:	Sales	EBITDA	Pre-Tax Profit	Net Profit	EPS	CF/S	Div.	Sales Growth	EBITDA Margin	Pre-ta x Margin	ROE
12/07E	45,061	4,364	n/a	1,758	24.2	n/a	10.00	-10.5%	9.7%	n/a	n/a
12/06E	50,326	3,900	n/a	2,125	29.5	n/a	10.30	7.9%	7.7%	n/a	n/a
12/05A	46,624	4,405	n/a	2,182	30.3	n/a	11.80	n/a	9.4%	n/a	n/a
12/04A	39,403	n/a	4,693	3,971	n/a	n/a	n/a	n/a	n/a	11.9%	21.0%
12/03A	29,567	n/a	1,577	1,386	n/a	n/a	n/a	n/a	n/a	5.3%	8.9%

Average Growth Rates:

	Sales	EBITDA	Pre-Tax Profit	Net Profit	EPS
05-07E	-2%	0%	n/a	-10%	-11%
03-05A	33%	n/a	198%	187%	n/a

VALUATION

P/E 12/07E	21.3x	Price/Book	1.3x
P/E 12/06E	17.3x	FV/EBITDA 12/06E	5.9x
Price/Revs 12/06E	0.2x	P/CFLO per share	n/a

BALANCE SHEET SUMMARY (as of 6/30/05)

Current assets	8,613.7	Current Liabilities	7,432.6
Fixed assets	20,143.4	Long-term debt	2,014.6
Other assets	0	Other liabilities	407.6
		Equity	18,902.3
Total assets	28,757.1	Total liab.s & equity	28,757.1
		L-T Debt/Capital	7.0%

SHARE DATA

Market cap (US$ mil.)	4,168	Avg. Daily Vol. (000)	258
Primary shares (mil.)	23.3	Avg. Daily Vol. ($ mn)	$ 13
Float (mil.)	n/a	Institutional ownership	2.6%
		Insider ownership	0.0%

RIEDEL RESEARCH GROUP INC OBJECTIVE EQUITY RESEARCH

Exhibit 4.4 Sinopec Shanghai Petrochemical Co. (Riedel Research Group, data from Reuters)

China Yuchai International Ltd

Country: China		Sector: Manufacturin g	
US Ticker	Price as of 02/21/06	52-week range:	Dividend:	Yield:
CYD	$8.99	$14.72-$7.12	$0.39	4.3%

COMPANY DESCRIPTION

China Yuchai International Ltd is a holding company that owns 76.4% of Yuchai. Yuchai is a medium-duty diesel engine manufacturer in China that also produces diesel power generators and diesel engine parts. Yuchai's primary products are medium-duty engines, which are principally used in trucks with a load capacity of five to seven tons. During 2004, the annual production capacity of Yuchai's manufacturing facilities was approximately 80,000 units of light-duty diesel engines, 120,000 units of medium-duty diesel engines and 50,000 units of heavy-duty diesel engines. Yuchai distributes its engines directly to auto plants and retailers from its primary manufacturing facilities in Yulin City. Yuchai provides a repair and replacement warranty for all of its engines. In March 2004, Yuchai established Yuchai Express Guarantee Company, to provide financing for Yuchai's customers to purchase its engines. In March 2005, the Company acquired 15% stake of TCL, a China-focused electronics distribution company.

SALES AND EARNINGS (in millions, except per-share data)

FY ends:	Sales	EBITDA	Pre-Tax Profit	Net Profit	EPS	CF/S	Div.		KEY RATIOS (%)			
								Sales Growth	EBITDA Margin	Pre-tax Margin	ROE
12/06E	1,125	283	108.7	63	1.69	1.18	0.45	143%	25.2%	9.7%	17.2%
12/05E	785	209	99.5	49	1.31	0.01	0.39	116%	26.6%	12.7%	15.2%
12/04E	674	206	91.1	59	1.68	0.13	0.39	122%	30.6%	13.5%	19.8%
12/03A	552	182.00	93.00	53.00	1.50	2.40	2.08	130%	33.0%	16.8%	22.0%
12/02A	424	152.00	85.98	50.00	1.41	1.66	0.19	n/a	35.8%	20.3%	19.1%

Average Growth Rates:

	Sales	EBITDA	Pre-Tax Profit
05-06E	43%	35%	29%
02-04A	29%	18%	10%

VALUATION

P/E 12/06E	5.3x	Price/Book	0.9x
P/E 12/05E	6.8x	FV/EBITDA 12/05E	1.5x
Price/Revs 12/05E	3.7x	P/CFLO per share	n/a

SHARE DATA

Market cap (US$ mil.)	292	Avg. Daily Vol. (000)	268
Primary shares (mil.)	35.4	Avg. Daily Vol. (US$)	$ 2,409
Float (mil.)	n/a	Institutional ownership	4.3%
		Insider ownership	n/a

BALANCE SHEET SUMMARY (as of 6/30/05)

Current assets	420	Current Liabilities	251
Fixed assets	140	Long-term debt	12
Other assets	90	Other liabilities	88
		Equity	300
Total assets	651	Total liab.s & equity	651
		L-T Debt/Capital	1.9%

RIEDEL RESEARCH GROUP INC OBJECTIVE EQUITY RESEARCH

Exhibit 4.5 China Yuchai International (Riedel Research Group, data from Reuters)

customers and industries that will benefit from having three times more refined fuel. One of the beneficiaries might be the $500 million market cap U.S.-listed China Yuchai (CYD), which specializes in manufacturing and distribution of diesel engines. This company might benefit from both the increased availability of refined fuel and the increase in economic and building activity generated by the project. Its diesel engines might be used as part of the construction or transportation for this plant, and its customers will definitely benefit from the local availability of more refined fuel. Also, the article mentions that the plant will have the capacity to produce petrochemicals including ethylene and polypropylene. As petroleum products, these petrochemicals (frequently used as the basic materials for plastics production) often go hand in hand with refinery projects. Considering the tremendous scale of China's economic growth, increased consumption of plastics is a given. One issue in China in recent years has, in fact, been the high prices of some of these plastic products. The dramatic increase in capacity for some of the basic ingredients in plastics could be good for Chinese consumers of these products who have been hurt by rising prices recently. One large and liquid possibility for a play on this trend is Chinese petrochemicals company Sinopec Shanghai Petrochemical. Sinopec not only produces petrochemicals themselves but also engages in the transportation and trade of petrochemicals on a broader scale. As a partner in this refinery venture, Sinopec Shanghai should benefit from these trends. See Exhibits 4.4 and 4.5.

Understand the Global Relationships

Understanding the relative position of countries and companies is as relevant in international investing as in understanding any other business situation. We'll come back to many of these relationships throughout the book, using them as examples of ideas and themes that people can invest in. This section outlines five or six themes that highlight the interaction, integration, and interreliance of several countries and economies around the world. At various times, these relationships provide investment opportunities. Sometimes they are of benefit to one country, sometimes to the other, but often to both. The important thing here is not so much these particular interrelationships but that you begin thinking about how to identify relationships that are somehow important to you because of your work, family, experience, or knowledge.

China and Brazil

Consider, for example, the relationship between growth in China and a Brazilian transportation logistics company. China's economy has been growing at a rate in the high single digits recently, driving demand for a multitude of products and raw materials. A significant portion of Brazil's economy is driven by tremendous raw materials reserves and agricultural production. In fact, the country is the second-largest producer (after the United States) of soybeans, while China is one of the world's major importers of soybeans—Chinese demand for soybeans more than doubled in 2005. Understanding the relationship between Chinese growth and imports from Brazil might get an investor interested in, say, the U.S. listing of a Brazilian transportation logistics company, América Latina Logística.

European Growth

Other relationships worth pondering are those being created by the growing integration of the various markets of Europe. An ever increasing number of European countries are working together to create a common market that is expected to eventually stretch from France to Lithuania. This will create opportunity for companies in smaller economies to tap into much larger markets. Companies will be able to capitalize on their particular strengths—manufacturing quality, access to skilled workers, cost advantages, and so on. There are 803 depository receipts for European companies that trade in the U.S. markets. Any one of these might provide the exposure that an investor is interested in and looking for. Consider banks, transportation companies (trucking, rail, shipping), and consumer goods companies. All of these will benefit in some way from having a larger market to finance, ship to, and sell to. Not all companies will be winners in this new environment, but it is important to recognize that the existence and growth of the European Union create additional opportunities, and some companies will be tremendous winners.

Mexico and the United States

Any American, especially anyone who grew up in the Southwest, knows very well the tight interaction and reliance of the U.S. economy—and society—on Mexico, and vice versa. The contributions in both directions are numerous, not only in popular culture but also in business and trade. While the relationship is sometimes rocky, everyone recognizes the interdependence of these two countries and economies. There are over a hundred Mexican companies and ADRs that trade in the United States. It is hard to imagine that any investor reading this book could not think of one trend that relies on this relationship between Mexico and the United States. Whether it's goods produced in the factories in northern Mexico, consumer products or media that come out of Mexico, or the chances for U.S. companies to sell into Mexico, the opportunities are numerous. Consider as well those Mexican companies that benefit from funds earned by Mexicans living and working in the United States that are sent back.

This concept of remittances is found in various

situations around the world. Many Filipinos, for example, work outside their country and send tremendous amounts of money back to the Philippines. This money is used by their families to build new homes and buy products, or it is saved in banks. The impact of this practice on an economy like Mexico's can be quite significant. In recent years, in fact, remittances have been the second most important source of foreign funds going into Mexico (after the petroleum industry). Remittances amount to over $12 billion per year—more than foreign direct investment and tourism. The opportunities for U.S. investors looking to participate in the benefits of this tremendous flow of money are numerous. Some of the areas to consider would be construction materials for all that new-home building, banks that benefit from all the fee income being generated, and consumer products companies that benefit from the increased disposable income of the recipients of these remittances.

Travel and Tourism

Having just gotten my one-year-old daughter a passport, I've been thinking a lot recently about travel. In the months following her first birthday, we intend to take our daughter to Australia, Fiji, and the United Kingdom. (Imagine that—traveling to three different countries before the age of one-and-a-half!) Little Ellie has also traveled across the United States five or six times in her young life. Just one generation ago, this amount of travel by a child would have been unheard of. In many countries, only now has the level of wealth and affluence climbed to the extent that people can consider buying travel and leisure with their extra disposable income.

There are nearly 70 global ADRs listed as travel and leisure plays. In the past few years, two Chinese companies, Ctrip and eLong, which focus on providing Internet-based travel services to the Chinese market, have listed in the United States. Ctrip has proven a much better investment than eLong, but over the long term both will likely be winners. Consider as well the Brazilian company Embraer. (If you have traveled recently, you may have flown on an Embraer jet.) Embraer dominates the market for smaller jets (in the 50- to 80-passenger range), which have become increasingly popular for direct flights to smaller cities in the United States and around the world.

Telephone and Internet Connections

As economies develop, communication becomes not only desirable but an absolute necessity. Over the past 10 or 15 years, we've all heard about the level of penetration of telephone or Internet connections in a developing economy. You often hear numbers such as the fact that 10, 15, or 20 percent of the population in a particular economy have a fixed-line telephone. But as with most statistics, there is another story just below the surface.

In China, for example, recent statistics show that fixed-line telephone penetration is about 25 percent nationwide. However, in cities such as Beijing and Shanghai, mobile phone penetration is as high as 90 percent. It is an often-told story that the telephone network in Cambodia is more advanced than that in the United States. The truth of the matter is that a fully digital cellular network was installed with the help of the US in the 1990s. So this network, though limited, was more advanced than the network in the United States, which still included a lot of analog (nondigital) infrastructure. There are many fascinating ways to invest in the prospects for greater penetration of phone and Internet connections in the developing world. Earlier, this book discussed using the Japanese telephone company as a way to play business growth in that economy. You might also consider using Telmex in Mexico, Net Serviços in Brazil, or VSNL in India as plays on the growth of connectivity in those countries. Consider as well using Swedish company Ericsson or Finnish company Nokia as a play on continued growth in mobile telephone services worldwide. By buying into these handset and network equipment companies, you are not making a bet on one particular country but on the idea that these companies will participate in the continued growth of cellular telephony. I think that's a pretty good bet.

Shipping and Trade

What drives interest in international investing are the scale, scope, and growth of international trade. Everywhere you look today you are surrounded by products that come from somewhere else. In fact, I just bought a bottle of water recently in New York City that came from Fiji. Pretty ridiculous that we are importing water from Fiji. But it is the reality of life today.

There are a number of companies worldwide that participate in trade. I'm not talking here about the companies that actually make clothing in Turkey, computers in Taiwan, or cars in Germany. I'm talking about the companies that move those products to other markets. If you think about it, everything that is manufactured needs to be financed, moved to the port, shipped, and smoothly delivered to the destination market. One of the markets that people think about immediately when considering trade is China. Over the past 20 years, China has become one of the major export powers in the world, exporting everything from paper to computer peripherals and from toys to technology products.

One interesting company that is a play on trade from China is Ninetowns Digital World Trade Holdings (NINE). This NASDAQ-listed software company specializes in the software needed to submit import-export documentation to the Chinese government electronically. In fact, for years they dominated this market with nearly 90 percent market share. However, this $300 million market cap Chinese company is not very well known by investors. While there been some changes in the company's business model (and I would encourage you to learn more about this company's current condition), it seems be well positioned to benefit from continued trade into and out of China—a fairly likely trend. Another industry that benefits from trade in general, but not in one particular commodity, is shipping. A quick look at any of the ADR web sites reveals that there are more than 50 industrial transport companies available to investors. Both air- and ocean-shipping stocks have been huge profit makers in recent years. Air transport has been a little bit trickier, due to the high fuel costs. Ocean shipping companies, such as Cosco Corp. in Singapore and Odfjell in Norway, have seen tremendous gains driven by the huge surge in worldwide transportation of goods in recent years.

The Death of Distance

With the explosive growth of the Internet and global telephony, one of the most impressive advances of the past decade has been what many call "the death of distance." It doesn't matter anymore whether you're sitting in the same office in the same town or even the same country, you can always collaborate and communicate by phone and Internet. Think about the last time you phoned the call center for your bank or a help line for a technology company. Chances are pretty high that you spoke to someone not in the United States but in China, India, or the Philippines. Wages are so much lower in those countries and because the cost of a phone call has come down to almost nothing, it's cheaper for those companies to connect you with a help line in India than to connect you with one in Oklahoma. The same holds true for software development and other business services.

When I was setting up my business a few years ago I used a web site called www.elance.com to do my graphic design, computer programming, web site design, and printing. It didn't matter to me where these people were sitting. My Microsoft Word document templates were built in Ireland, my brochures printed in Pakistan, my logo designed in Argentina, and my web site built in Houston, Texas. I work with these people through e-mail, instant messaging, and telephone. I probably would have done the same thing even if they had been here in New York City. I did not need to meet them face-to-face.

Big companies have discovered the same thing I learned when I was setting up my modest company. You can find the best talents in the world—literally all over the world—and work with them online. Many American businesses started by moving their call center operations to countries like India and have since begun to have Indian computer programmers and engineers build their software and design their products. The U.S. listings of Indian information technology (IT) outsourcing companies such as Infosys, Satyam, and Wipro provide a way to invest in this trend. So the next time you pick up the phone and your call to a U.S. company's 800 number ends up in Southeast Asia somewhere, think about the opportunity to invest in that trend. With luck, the customer service person will be able to solve your problem at the same time.

Banking Innovations

When was the last time you wrote a check? Remember how often you used to get your checkbook out? I know that in our house we write a few checks per month to pay certain bills, but most of our banking is either done online or somehow connected to credit/debit cards. Looking around the world, you'll find that countries are in various stages of a revolution in the way they pay for stuff. In some countries in Western Europe, for example, you can use your mobile phone today for time on a parking meter or coffee at the local cafe. You work with the service to upload value to the computer chip in your mobile phone and a reader on a street corner or the shop counter reduces the value by what you spend. Pretty fancy.

In other countries, most transactions still use cash, and credit/debit cards are not widespread. It is amazing, however, how quickly that can change. In the late 1990s, governments in South Korea and China started to encourage widespread use of credit cards. In both cases, the near-term reason for this government effort was to build credit card use and infrastructure ahead of major sporting events that were coming to their countries. Unfortunately, in South Korea, consumers went a little crazy, encouraged by a tax deduction on credit card purchases (imagine that!). Credit card spending went up 500 percent between 1998 and 2002. Total outstanding debt on credit cards grew from $11 billion in 1999 to nearly $60 billion in late 2003. Eventually, borrowers defaulted on about quarter of that debt.

Hopefully having learned from South Korea's example, China is now embarking on a similar push to grow credit card adoption in preparation for the Olympics in Beijing in 2008. A state-run credit payments company is building massive credit card infrastructure. By some estimates there are 100 million credit cards currently in use in China, accounting for less than 2 percent of private spending. Expect to see winners and losers in this business, but we can be quite sure that we will see strong growth in credit card use and adoption around the world in coming years. Carefully choosing investments in China's banking sector might be a way to play this trend. Also consider smaller banks in Hong Kong and AEON Credit Service Co. in Japan. This company, listed in New York through the ADR (AONNY), provides a way to play growth throughout Asia through its subsidiaries in Thailand, Hong Kong, Singapore, and other Asian countries. There are certain risks in this business, but this company's shares are up 30 percent year to date and it looks set for continued strong growth.

Once again, I am not suggesting that you play these trends but that you use this process as a way to help you identify trends that are appropriate for you, are aligned with your interests, and seem compelling. This is not meant to be a series of investment ideas but a set of tools and a process to help you develop your own ideas.

Chapter FIVE

Invest in Line with Government Goals

Over the past few years, I've become increasingly surprised at how often professional fund managers ignore what I consider to be one of the basic tenets of investing. Throughout this book I've reminded investors that business models around the world and investment opportunities in those business models are pretty much the same no matter what country they operate in. Remember the example of Google. Not a lot of investors understand the technical details of Google's search engine, but they do understand the dollars and cents that Google delivers to the bottom line quarter after quarter and year after year. Similarly, you don't need to know the details of the technology a Turkish cellular company is using to believe in the fact that a well-run company in Turkey that happens to provide mobile service is going to benefit from continued growth in the Turkish economy and the rising wealth of the Turkish consumer. But if the Turkish government comes out and makes some dramatic proclamation about how it doesn't want to have cellular service in the country, we, as investors, should listen and probably not invest in cellular. Although this is an outrageous example, governments provide insights like this all the time. I'm shocked at how often investors (even professionals) ignore them.

Chapter 7 discusses why it's crucial to know the personalities involved in your companies and how those personalities relate to the government and the political powers that be. This chapter focuses more on general trends in government policies and how they can impact your investment.

Most American investors seem to think that the role of government in investing is to get out of the way. In a truly capitalist system, the government stays well out of the way of the entrepreneurs and businesspeople who make industry and business run. But in reality, even here in the United States, which is largely a free-market economy, government decisions, policies, and actions can have a big impact on investors. For example, a stronger or weaker Food and Drug Administration (FDA) can have a major effect on food and pharmaceutical companies. The action of a newly powerful FDA to dramatically ramp up its oversight and control of pharmaceutical companies would have a serious impact on the value of the prescription drug pipeline for an individual pharmaceutical company. Investors need to know if it's going to take three years to get a drug to market rather than one year and appropriately discount the value of those future earnings in consideration of for the delay.

One interesting example of this occurred in 2004. Following Janet Jackson's revealing performance at the Super Bowl in early 2004, the role of the Federal Communications Commission (FCC) in monitoring the decency of what goes out over public airwaves was highlighted and examined. In this particular case, both the network that broadcast the Super Bowl (CBS) and the company that organized Janet Jackson's halftime show (MTV) are part of widely held public company, Viacom. CBS ended up being fined $550,000 by the FCC, the largest fine ever levied against a TV network. While not a perfect example, this case does serve to emphasize the fact that even in a country like the United States, where government typically stays well away from business activities, it is still worthwhile for investors to consider the impact of government wishes and actions.

As you can imagine, in other countries government beliefs and actions have an even greater impact on the outlook for particular businesses, sectors, and industries. Western European governments, for example, are well known for limiting the ability of a business to fire workers at will. In France, for example, companies routinely report that it is very difficult to let workers go. This has, in fact, led to widespread use in France of temporary employment agencies, where the workers aren't officially employed by the company but are used on an as-needed basis. Investors need to take this type of situation into consideration when investing in a cyclical company where a slowdown or downturn might lead to the desire to reduce the workforce. In a country where government policy makes it difficult to let workers go, the company could be hindered in its ability to be flexible with its workforce.

Governments routinely give us useful insights into their views about companies, industries, and sectors. One country where this kind of information is tremendously useful is China. The Chinese government issues a five-year plan that outlines its intentions for economic and social development over the next five years. As of the writing of this book, the government had just announced its eleventh five-year plan, covering the period from 2006 through 2010.

Three central tenets of this plan are crucial for investors to keep in mind. First, the government has said it intends to raise rural incomes to close the gap between poorer rural areas and wealthier urban areas. It's not hard to imagine how a government would go about encouraging rising rural incomes. Facilitating transport of goods to market, tinkering with the tax code, investing government resources in agricultural innovations, and so on, are ways the strong central government might put into practice its intention of raising rural incomes. Having followed international investments for many years, I have noticed time and time again that whenever rural incomes rise, certain types of companies seem to benefit. In particular, fertilizer companies, motorcycle companies, and agricultural equipment companies benefit from rising rural incomes. It's not hard to imagine that a wealthier farmer is going to end up spending more on fertilizer and agricultural equipment. If any money is left over, that farmer may want to buy a motorcycle or some other relatively high-priced item that he may have been holding out to purchase. This pattern has been seen throughout Asia and Latin America.

Now that the Chinese government is focusing on raising rural incomes, we may want to look at some opportunities to invest in these areas. Two ideas that come to mind are Bodisen Biotech and General Steel Holdings. Bodisen, listed on the AMEX, is a small-cap company that specializes in organic fertilizer in China. General Steel Holdings is a U.S.-listed Chinese steel company that specializes in thin sheets of metal used for agricultural equipment and machinery. See Exhibits 5.1 and 5.2.

The second facet of the Chinese five-year plan that needs to be taken into consideration is the government's desire to develop the western part of the country. Much of the Chinese development that we hear about in the news and see on TV relates to the very wealthy and fast-growing coastal and southern areas of China. Shanghai, Guangzhou, and Shenzhen are all cities that have benefited tremendously from the growing industrialization

General Steel Holdings

Country: United States		Sector: Steel	

US Ticker	Price as of 02/21/06	52-week range:	Dividend:	Yield:
GSHO.OB	$1.95	$1.95-$0.98	$0.00	0.0%

COMPANY DESCRIPTION

The Group's principal activity is manufacturing hot rolled carbon and silicon steel sheets that are mainly used on tractors, agricultural vehicles and in other specialty markets. "Qiu Steel" is the registered trademark under which the Group sells its products. The Group sells its products primarily to distributors, service centers or manufacturers who further process these products.

SALES AND EARNINGS (in thousands, except per-share data) / **KEY RATIOS (%)**

FY ends:	Sales	EBITDA	Pre-Tax Profit	Net Profit	EPS	CF/S	Div.	Sales Growth	EBITDA Margin	Pre-tax Margin	ROE
12/07E	308.6	16.5	10.7	5.7	0.18	n/a	0.00	13.3%	5.3%	3.5%	24.3%
12/06E	272.5	16.3	10.4	6.5	0.21	n/a	0.00	104.7%	6.0%	3.8%	37.7%
12/05E	133.1	11.7	7.9	4.9	0.16	n/a	0.00	51.6%	8.8%	6.0%	41.9%
12/04A	87.8	5.1	2.3	0.9	0.03	n/a	0.00	53.3%	5.8%	2.6%	10.5%
12/03A	57.3	n/a	2.3	1.1	0.03	n/a	0.00	n/a	n/a	4.1%	14.4%
Average Growth Rates:											
05-07E	52%	19%	16%	8%	6%						
03-04A	53%	n/a	-2%	-16%	0%						

VALUATION

P/E 12/07E	7.1x	Price/Book	n/a
P/E 12/06E	6.2x	FV/EBITDA 12/06E	n/a
Price/Revs 12/06E	0.0x	P/CFLO per share	n/a

BALANCE SHEET SUMMARY (as of 6/30/05)

Current assets	49,009	Current Liabilities	54,935
Fixed assets	36,842	Long-term debt	0
Other assets	1,990	Other liabilities	18,813
		Equity	14,094
Total assets	87,842	Total liab.s & equity	87,842
		L-T Debt/Capital	0.0%

SHARE DATA

Market cap (US$ mil.)	63	Avg. Daily Vol. (000)	57.4
Primary shares (mil.)	32.4	Avg. Daily Vol. (US$) $	112
Float (mil.)	n/a	Institutional ownership	n/a
		Insider ownership	78.0%

RIEDEL RESEARCH GROUP INC OBJECTIVE EQUITY RESEARCH

Exhibit 5.1 General Steel Holdings
(Riedel Research Group, data from Reuters)

Bodisen Biotech

Country: United States	Sector: Agriculture and Manufacturing	
US Ticker	Price as of 02/21/06	
BBC	$15.05	

52-week range:	Dividend:	Yield:
$21.3-$5.06		

COMPANY DESCRIPTION

Bodisen Biotech, Inc. (Bodisen), manufactures and markets organic fertilizers and pesticides to 20 agricultural provinces of China. The Company also conducts research and development to improve its products, and develops new formulas and products. Bodisen maintains over 60 packaged products. Organic Compound Fertilizers have been found to increase yields within one planting season in a variety of crops, including, wheat, maize, tobacco, and various vegetable and fruit crops. Plants tend to easily absorb organic fertilizer without the side effects found in synthetic chemical fertilizer products. The Company has developed a series of liquid fertilizers that can be applied to grapes, pears, cucumbers, potatoes, watermelon, apples, oranges, asparagus, garlic and strawberries. Liquid fertilizer heightens the color and luster of fruits and vegetables, and the overall quality of the end product. The Company's pesticide and insecticide products can be applied to fruit trees and vegetable crops, and help eliminate harmful pests that reduce overall crop yields.

128

	SALES AND EARNINGS (in millions, except per-share data)							KEY RATIOS (%)			
			Pre-tax	Net				Sales	EBITDA	Pre-tax	
FY ends:	Sales	EBITDA	Profit	Profit	EPS	CF/S	Div.	Growth	Margin	Margin	ROE
12/07E	49.6	n/a	n/a	n/a	0.91	n/a	0.00	69.9%	n/a	n/a	n/a
12/06E	29.2	n/a	n/a	n/a	0.55	n/a	0.00	421.4%	n/a	n/a	n/a
12/05E	5.6	n/a	n/a	n/a	0.09	n/a	0.00	-65.5%	n/a	n/a	n/a
12/04A	16.2	n/a	5.03	5.03	n/a	n/a	0.00	66.0%	n/a	31.0%	37.4%
12/03A	9.8	n/a	1.97	1.97	n/a	n/a	0.00	n/a	n/a	20.1%	20.6%

Average Growth Rates:

05-07E	198%	n/a	n/a	n/a	115%
03-05A	66%	n/a	155%	155%	n/a

VALUATION

P/E 12/07E	17.3x	Price/Book	16.5x
P/E 12/06E	44.4	FV/EBITDA 12/06E	30.1x
Price/Revs 12/06E	116.6	P/CFLO per share	14.4x

BALANCE SHEET SUMMARY (as of 6/30/05)

Current assets	9.6	Current Liabilities	1.4
Fixed assets	5.2	Long-term debt	
Other assets	-	Other liabilities	
		Equity	13.4
Total assets	14.8	Total liab.s & equity	14.8
		L-T Debt/Capital	0.0%

SHARE DATA

Market cap (US$ mil.)	232.9	Avg. Daily Vol. (000)	0.35
Primary shares (mil.)	15.5	Avg. Daily Vol. (US$)	$ 5.3
Float (mil.)	n/a	Institutional ownership	11.0%
		Insider ownership	47.0%

RIEDEL RESEARCH GROUP INC OBJECTIVE EQUITY RESEARCH

Exhibit 5.2 Bodisen Biotech
(Riedel Research Group, data from Reuters)

129

and urbanization of the Chinese economy and population. Many observers fail to realize, however, that focusing on the thin coastal strip ignores the very large and
populous interior of China. Some 900 million of China's
1.3 billion population live in rural communities, often
far from the glitz and glamour of the skylines of Shanghai and Shenzhen. Having such a bifurcated population
can be a problem for a strong central government. Massive movements of migrant workers in China in recent
years have strained the social fabric and the equity of
wealthy coastal areas versus poorer inland areas.

This situation is on its way to becoming untenable
in modern China. Once again, it's not hard to imagine
what a government might do to balance economic development. In addition to putting roadblocks in the way of
continued development of coastal areas, the Chinese
government can build infrastructure and educational
facilities and make adjustments to its spending and tax-
ing to encourage development in the western part of the
country. Physical infrastructure can be crucial for economic development. As a play on this in China, I would
focus on building materials companies, railway companies, and toll-road companies. Crucial links between a
rural population and the urban markets that they serve
are the physical railways and roadways to bring products
to market. In China, I might focus on Guangshen Railway as a play on this theme. See Exhibit 5.3.

Finally, the Chinese government has made it a top

priority to balance environmental protection and economic growth. Over the last 50 years, the focus in China has been very firmly on economic growth—and to great success. What has suffered, however, is the environment. Stories of notorious air pollution, widespread chemical spills, and significant national projects, such as the Three Gorges Dam, have provided evidence that the priority in China has been economic rather than environmental. That the government would include in such an important strategic document as the five-year plan a comment about the necessity of balancing environmental protection with economic growth is certainly worth noting. The companies that will benefit from the increased focus on environmental protection are alternative energy companies that provide cleaner-burning fuel or cleaner energy sources and wastewater treatment companies that can help to treat industrial wastewater before it is introduced into the environment.

Fortunately for the U.S. investor, many plays on this theme are available in the United States. The listing of Suntech power in late 2005 benefited greatly from the increased interest in alternative energy (in this case, solar). Other companies such as Far East Energy, a U.S.-listed small-cap play on coal-bed methane gas, might also be of interest. On the wastewater treatment side, most of the companies are listed in Singapore and Hong Kong, but some future listing will surely provide some exposure. See Exhibits 5.4 and 5.5.

Guangshen Railway Co Ltd

Country: China	Sector: Transportation		
US Ticker	Price as of 02/21/06	52-week range:	Dividend:	Yield:
GSH	$16.25	$13.10-$20.74	$0.66	4.1%

COMPANY DESCRIPTION

Guangshen Railway Co. provides railway passenger and freight transportation services between Guangzhou and Shenzhen, and certain long-distance passenger transportation services. Its freight services include the transportation of cargo, and containers. The company also sells food, beverages, and merchandise aboard its trains and in its stations; as well as engaging in advertising; tourism; and property leasing. As of 2004, it operated 117 pairs of passenger trains per day, of which 64 pairs were high-speed passenger trains operating between Guangzhou and Shenzhen; 2 were regular-speed passenger trains operating between Guangzhou and Shenzhen; 13 were Hong Kong through-trains; and 38 were domestic long-distance passenger trains. As of the same date, there were 26 stations situated on its rail line, providing services for cities, towns, and ports situated between Guangzhou and Shenzhen in the Guangzhou-Shenzhen corridor, and Hong Kong.

132

SALES AND EARNINGS (in millions, except per-share data)

FY ends:	Sales	EBITDA	Pre-Tax Profit	Net Profit	EPS	CF/S	Div.
12/06E	429	140	n/a	88	1.01	0.93	0.81
12/05E	405	130	n/a	79	0.92	0.78	0.73
12/04A	367	117	n/a	69	0.79	1.29	0.66
12/03A	298	103	n/a	62.0	0.71	0.64	0.63
12/02A	314	116	n/a	67.0	0.78	0.84	0.60

KEY RATIOS (%)

	Sales Growth	EBITDA Margin	Pre-tax Margin	ROE
12/06E	5.9%	32.6%	n/a	6.7%
12/05E	10.4%	32.1%	n/a	6.2%
12/04A	23.2%	31.9%	n/a	5.4%
12/03A	-5.1%	34.6%	n/a	5.0%
12/02A	n/a	36.9%	n/a	5.4%

Average Growth Rates:

	Sales	EBITDA	Pre-Tax Profit
05-07E	6%	7%	10%
03-05A	8%	0%	1%

VALUATION

P/E 12/05E	16.0x	Price/Book	1.1x
P/E 12/05E	17.7x	FV/EBITDA 12/05E	10.8
Price/Revs 112/05E	0.04x	P/CFLO per share	20.9

BALANCE SHEET SUMMARY (as of 6/30/05)

Current assets	361	Current Liabilities	113
Fixed assets	843	Long-term debt	0
Other assets	175	Other liabilities	6
		Net Worth	1,260
Total assets	1,380	Total liab.s & equity	1,380
		L-T Debt/Capital	0.0%

SHARE DATA

Market cap (US$ mil.)	1,409	Avg. Daily Vol. (000)	14.6
Primary shares (mil.)	86.7	Avg. Daily Vol. (US$)	$ 237
Float (mil.)	n/a	Institutional ownership	0.9%
		Insider ownership	n/a

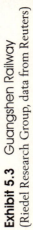

RIEDEL RESEARCH GROUP INC OBJECTIVE EQUITY RESEARCH

Exhibit 5.3 Guangshen Railway
(Riedel Research Group, data from Reuters)

133

Far East Energy Corp

Country: China		Sector: Energy	
US Ticker	Price as of 02/21/06		
FEEC.OB	$1.99		
		52-week range:	Dividend:	Yield:
		$2.20 - $0.86	$0.00	0.0%

COMPANY DESCRIPTION

Far East Energy Corporation, incorporated on February 4, 2000, is a development-stage company focused on coalbed methane (CBM) in the People's Republic of China. The Company has entered into three production sharing contracts that enable it to explore for, develop, produce and sell CBM on over 1.3 million acres located in the Yunnan and Shanxi Provinces of the PRC. As of December 31, 2004, FEEC has drilled three exploratory wells in Yunnan Province and completed a hydraulic fracture simulation test on a well in Shanxi Province. In Feb 05, the Company sold its oil and gas leasehold interests and other property interests in Montana which it considers non-core assets.

134

	SALES AND EARNINGS (in millions, except per-share data)							KEY RATIOS (%)			
FY ends:	Sales	Oper. Income	Pre-Tax Profit	Net Profit	EPS	CF/S	Div.	Sales Growth	EBITDA Margin	Pre-tax Margin	ROE
12/07E	n/a	n/a	n/a	n/a	n/a	n/a	0.00	n/a	n/a	n/a	n/a
12/06E	n/a	n/a	n/a	n/a	n/a	n/a	0.00	n/a	n/a	n/a	n/a
12/05A	0.0	(8)	(8)	(8)	(13.00)	n/a	0.00	n/a	n/a	n/a	-75.0%
12/04A	0.0	(7)	(7)	(7)	(12.00)	n/a	0.00	n/a	n/a	n/a	-55.0%
12/03A	14.0	(2)	(2)	(2)	(4.00)	n/a	0.00	n/a	n/a	n/a	-192.0%
Average Growth Rates:											
05-07E	n/a	n/a	n/a	n/a	n/a	n/a					
03-05A	n/a	n/a	n/a	n/a	n/a	n/a					

VALUATION			
P/E 12/07E	n/a	Price/Book	9.0x
P/E 12/06E	n/a	FV/EBITDA 12/06E	n/a
Price/Revs 12/06E	n/a	P/CFLO per share	n/a

BALANCE SHEET SUMMARY (as of 6/30/05)			
Current assets	13	Current Liabilities	3
Fixed assets	8	Long-term debt	0
Other assets	0	Other liabilities	0
		Equity	19
Total assets	22	Total liab.s & equity	22
		L-T Debt/Capital	0.0%

SHARE DATA			
Market cap (US$ mil.)	201	Avg. Daily Vol. (000)	371
Primary shares (mil.)	96.8	Avg. Daily Vol. (US$)	$ 742
Float (mil.)	n/a	Institutional ownership	26.0%
		Insider ownership	16.0%

RIEDEL
RESEARCH GROUP INC OBJECTIVE EQUITY RESEARCH

Exhibit 5.4 Far East Energy Corp.
(Riedel Research Group, data from Reuters)

Suntech

Country: China	Sector: Energy		
US Ticker	Price as of 02/21/06	52-week range:	Dividend:	Yield:
STP	$37.70	$19 - $45.95	$0.00	0.0%

COMPANY DESCRIPTION

Suntech Power Holdings Co., Ltd., incorporated on August 8, 2005, is a solar energy company designing, developing, manufacturing and marketing a range of photovoltaic (PV) cells and modules, which are devices that convert sunlight into electricity through a process known as the photovoltaic effect. It also provides PV system integration services in China. Its products are used to provide electric power for residential, commercial, industrial and public utility applications in a range of markets worldwide, including a number of European countries, such as Germany and Spain, as well as China and the United States. It sells its products outside of China primarily through distributors, and in China primarily to end users directly. During the year ended December 31, 2004, the Company sold 92.2% of its products to customers outside of China. The Company derives its revenues from three sources - sales of PV modules account for over 90% of revenues in 2004.

SALES AND EARNINGS (in millions, except per-share data)

FY ends:	Sales	EBITDA	Pre-Tax Profit	Net Profit	EPS	CF/S	Div.	Sales Growth	EBITDA Margin	Pre-tax Margin	ROE
										KEY RATIOS (%)	
12/07E	971.50	n/a	n/a	n/a	1.18	n/a	0.00	76.6%	n/a	n/a	n/a
12/06E	550.00	n/a	n/a	n/a	0.66	n/a	0.00	143.4%	n/a	n/a	n/a
12/05A	226.00	n/a	34.29	30.60	0.31	n/a	0.00	165.0%	n/a	15.2%	n/a
12/04A	85.29	n/a	19.20	19.81	0.22	n/a	0.00	514.0%	n/a	22.5%	72.1%
12/03A	13.89	n/a	0.62	0.93	n/a	n/a	0.00	n/a	n/a	4.5%	13.7%

Average Growth Rates:

	Sales	Pre-Tax Profit	Net Profit	EPS
06-07E	77%	n/a	n/a	79%
03-05A	303%	644%	474%	n/a

VALUATION

P/E 12/07E	199.1x	Price/Book	125.7x
P/E 12/06E	250.7	FV/EBITDA 12/06E	64.0x
Price/Revs 12/06E	n/a	P/CFLO per share	n/a

SHARE DATA

Market cap (US$ mil.)	5,454	Avg. Daily Vol. (000)	2.74
Primary shares (mil.)	144.7	Avg. Daily Vol. (US$)	$ 103
Float (mil.)	n/a	Institutional ownership	15.0%
		Insider ownership	n/a

BALANCE SHEET SUMMARY (as of 6/30/05)

Current assets	436.0	Current Liabilities	72.0
Fixed assets	39.7	Long-term debt	3.7
Other assets	1.9	Other liabilities	-
		Equity	401.9
Total assets	477.6	Total liab.s & equity	477.6
		L-T Debt/Capital	0.8%

RIEDEL
RESEARCH GROUP INC OBJECTIVE EQUITY RESEARCH

Exhibit 5.5 Suntech
(Riedel Research Group, data from Reuters)

Moves by the South African government to increase local Black management in corporations, by the Korean government to ensure that the economy continually moves up the scale from manufacturing cheap plastic toys to being a world leader in computer chips, and the high-profile involvement of Brazilian government officials in satisfying Chinese demand for many of the agricultural and mineral imports from that country are great examples of themes that investors can use to invest in accordance with government wishes. It goes without saying that you should avoid investing in sectors, industries, and companies that are on the wrong side of this trend as well. If the government has made it clear that it doesn't want the expansion of a certain industry or doesn't like the products or services of a certain company, investors in that opportunity are fighting an uphill battle. With attractive investment opportunities around the world, why bother investing against government wishes?

Chapter SIX

Don't Buy Regulatory Structure

When you are investing overseas, remember that the regulatory environment is likely quite different from that in the U.S. Government in the U.S. largely runs on the philosophy that the market should be allowed to function freely and most goods and services be delivered by business. While certain regulations are necessary to protect consumer safety and to ensure certain public goods (education, electricity, transport, and so on), much of the rest of business activity is left to the forces of the market. However, in other countries at various stages of development, government has played a more significant role in driving and determining business activity. In the early stages of economic growth in countries like Korea, Taiwan, and Singapore, the government clearly determined which industries would be favored for development. The successful migration of the economy of Taiwan, for example, from making cheap toys in the 1960s to making computer chips in the 1990s was in some ways managed by the government. Tax breaks, policies, and government initiatives encouraged development of the various industries.

The role of the government often involves either the direct protection of domestic industry or the provision of certain things that are seen as necessary for economic growth with regard to the protection of domestic industry. Citizens of every country will be familiar with this idea. The United States has, at various times, tried to protect its steel industry, textile workers, and farmers from the vagaries of the world market. We often think of the United States as a free-trade country, but various tariffs and protections to protect domestic manufacturers make it clear that that's not entirely true. In countries like Malaysia, for example, the government has tried to encourage the development of a domestic automotive industry. This has required high tariffs on the import of cars from other countries. This strategy has met with some success and has helped to develop the homegrown capability to manufacture and distribute automotive parts. However, the opening of a market to eventual foreign competition is always somewhere on the horizon. Governments always focus on setting a certain amount of time—a certain number of years—during which domestic industry will be protected. At the end of that time, the market is opened up and, hopefully, the domestic players will have become strong enough to fend for themselves in the face of foreign competition. This is one of the goals of the World Trade Organization (WTO), which aims to lower tariff and nontariff barriers around the world. A country such as China, which is joining the WTO, has had to agree to a certain timetable to allow total competition in industries like banking, telecom, and insurance.

Opening an industry to competition is likely to have several consequences. In the United States, the swift deregulation of the airline industry and the telephone industry has meant lower prices for consumers and a host of new services. There are trade-offs, including the elimination of many high-wage jobs and, often, the reduction in strength of employee unions. Some companies in many industries that are nonunion are benefiting from lower wages and avoiding legacy problems in pension plans, benefits, and so on. From an investment point of view, a number of new opportunities typically turn up when markets open up, as new entrants need to raise capital and look for investors.

It is the government's role in almost every society to provide the basic public utilities for that society to function and grow. These *public goods* include such things as transportation infrastructure, and utilities. Some of these are provided by government directly (education, in most cases), but in many situations the government realizes that it doesn't have the resources (financial or in terms of expertise) to develop these services. Often in such situations, the government grants a particular company a

141

monopoly for a certain number of years in exchange for building out the required infrastructure. In Thailand, for example, the government instituted a program of "Build Transfer Operate" concessions to drive the development of telecom service infrastructure. Because regulations specified that only the government could own telecom networks, private companies were required to build the networks and then transfer ownership to the government. In exchange for their investment and commitment, the companies were allowed to operate the networks for 25 or 30 years. In some countries, the government has simply decided to keep for itself the monopoly on a particular service, whether that be the distribution of electricity, phone service, or toll roads, and then turn to the capital markets to raise the money for the required build-out.

Unfortunately, technology and trade usually move much faster than government bureaucrats. In the case of a tariff to protect a particular industry, it is often true that a product or service developed without proper competition will suffer. Factories and manufacturers in the former Soviet Union were notorious for producing plenty of products, but nothing that people wanted to buy. Given the pace, ease, and flow of international trade today, protecting domestic industry is very hard. It seems inevitable, whether through smuggling or consumers simply choosing to use different products, that subpar products won't have a very long shelf life. The market often finds a way around these artificial official barriers well before the government realizes that the domestic industry and its beloved tariff is past its sell-by date.

Businesses that operate behind a wall of government protection typically have not made very good investments. Those companies are not required by the market to make good investments with their money or ensure that they keep up with the demands of the market. They often have too many employees, are too political, and spend too much of their time worrying about maintaining their protection rather than developing their products and their market. Businesses in some way related to technology have an even bigger problem. The death of distance (discussed in Chapter 4) and

Mexican Radio

One simple example of the effect of government regulation comes from my youth in Southern California, where radio stations were established on the Mexican side of the border to avoid having to comply with FCC regulations. These companies set transmitters that reached well over the border into the United States, but they were able to do as they pleased rather than worry about FCC regulations. For an hour every Sunday evening, these radio stations would play Spanish-language Mexican cultural programs that would not have been heard otherwise. I haven't kept up with FCC regulations, but I know that over time, the regulations were moderated. Part of the reason may well have been the presence of these radio stations on the Mexican side of the border.

the widespread availability of information have made it virtually impossible for a technology company to remain protected for long.

Plenty of New Technologies Impact Investment

Think for a moment about the impact of satellites on TV and radio broadcasting or TiVo on the habits of people watching television. Consider the effect of the Internet on the way people communicate. These are good examples of how technology, often driven by market forces, moved much faster than government regulations ever could. It seems that the government is often in the position of trying to make their regulations 'catch up' with the realities of the world. Often the market has moved to correct or adjust whatever the government is trying to control well before the government gets around to making the necessary changes. In this chapter I will go through a few examples to illustrate the impact of trade, technology and government regulation on investment opportunities.

The title of this chapter is "Don't Buy Regulatory Structure." This subject is something to keep in mind when choosing your actual investments. You're better off owning something tested by market forces than something that relies on an artificial barrier or protection to succeed. Political will is fickle. And technology and trade are very powerful forces. The impact of these forces on an inefficient and ineffective company can be serious.

International Monopoly? I Don't Think So . . .

While I was working for Salomon Brothers, which eventually morphed into Salomon Smith Barney, I worked on the public offering of shares in Videsh Sanchar Nigam Ltd. (VSNL) in the mid 1990s, when the company had the exclusive monopoly on all international telephone traffic into and out of India. The government had held onto the right to control every bit of sound going over the wires into and out of India. Investors all over the word looked at this and thought, "This is too good to be true." And they were right. The need of the 1 billion people in India to be connected with the rest of the world accelerated in the 1990s well beyond the ability of this one company to provide service. There were not enough international circuits to fill the need for international connectivity.

On the one hand, VSNL looked like a great opportunity, the exclusive provider of international telephony and connectivity to a fast-growing nation. In addition, the company even had an agreement with the government that fixed the amount it would earn and adjusted it for changes in currency and in the rate it received from other telephone companies around the world (settlement rates). At the time of the issue in the late 1990s, settlement rates were plummeting in most markets as a result of deregulation. VSNL did indeed have the monopoly on international traffic into and out of India, but the market correctly predicted that it would

145

not last until 2004 as had been promised during the listing of the global depository receipts (GDRs) in the late
1990s. The government finally gave up in 2002 and
ended the monopoly. The company was given the right
to enter the long-distance market, but by then the dam-
age had been done. The shares that had traded at Rs416
in 1997 fell to Rs70 in early 2003. There has been a nice
recovery since, but those investors who were telling me
in 1997 that the VSNL monopoly story was "too good
to be true" have been proven right. The shares had fallen
by 83 percent. See Figure 6.1.

Because of its place at the crossroads of development, emerging technology, and government regulation,
telecom provides many examples of the breakdown of a
regulatory system. At the same time I was working on
the VSNL deal, I was living in Bangkok, where the cost
for a telephone call to the United States was nearly $2
per minute. When a five-minute telephone call home

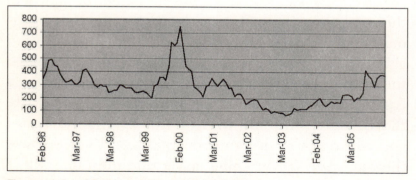

Figure 6.1 GDR Share Price (2001–2006)

costs $10, you're bound to look for some sort of alternative. Some ingenious entrepreneur decided that there was a way to provide a U.S. dial tone to residents of other countries through a very creative callback system. I forget how I first heard about this, but it was likely from another ex-pat feeling the pain of those high telephone bills. It worked this way: You would call a designated number in the United States, wait for a ring, and then hang up (before the call connected and there was any charge). A few seconds later, your phone would ring and when you picked it up, there was the familiar hum of a dial tone. You would simply dial the number you wanted and it was as though you were dialing from within the United States, with all the associated low call charges.

It was a bit of a cat-and-mouse game to keep this system running because the Communications Authority of Thailand (CAT, the government telephone company that held the monopoly for international telephony) would try to jam the numbers that the service was using. No problem—there was always a fax on my machine the next morning with a new list of numbers. I remember going to meetings at this time to talk to the CAT about how wonderful it would be for it to go public (at the time, I was working for Salomon Smith Barney as an equity analyst) and thinking in the back of my mind that the technological advances that I was taking advantage of were the death knell for the company. Seven years later, they are no closer to going public and the value of the entity has been destroyed by technological advances.

Similar situations in which technology trumps government regulation appear quite frequently to this day. The main culprit recently has been Voice over Internet Protocol (VoIP) calls. VoIP allows users to make telephone calls over the Internet, thus avoiding the very high tariffs for international calls that can exist in many countries around the world. In mid-2005, the African countries of Ghana and Kenya tried to stop the hemorrhaging of their international call revenue by closing all outgoing Internet lines of Internet service providers (ISPs). In Ghana, the telecom monopoly was complaining that its international call business had dropped from a profit of $42 million in 1999 to a loss of $14 million in 2004. This dramatic loss in income is bound to get the government's attention; the revenue from international calls can be quite significant to a smaller economy.

You may feel somewhat sorry for these legacy providers being left behind as technology changes rapidly around them—but you don't have to invest in them.

The moral of this story is that you should avoid regulatory structure and monopolies that could be changed or undermined by evolving technology.

The same goes for tariffs. I would never invest in a company whose livelihood is determined by the existence of a tariff barrier. Whether it is a textile company in a country that is not competitive in that industry or a company that benefits from government subsidies on some input (oil, coal, diesel, . . .), the first whiff of economic distress or even a change in political leadership can change that very quickly, and the value of your investment will decline with it.

Votes of Steel

In 2002 and 2003, the Bush administration in the United States decided to pander to steelworkers (read: voters) by instituting tariffs on steel products. The argument was that steel was being produced in countries like China, Korea, and Russia and then dumped on the world market at prices below the cost of production. What was really happening was that the prices were lower than what the U.S. businesses could make steel for. The complaints told us more about the U.S. steel industry than about the appropriate price for steel in the world market. The tariffs were lifted after about 18 months because a case brought by Europe was poised to move through the court of the World Trade Organization (WTO), and the United States was certain to lose.

Think about what the free market would have done in this situation. The market would have fixed the problem in time. If these companies and countries were truly selling steel at below cost, they would have gone out of business, reducing the supply of steel and driving up prices. Instead, the U.S. steel industry insisted on and was granted tariffs, which lasted conveniently through the presidential election. They were allowed to expire a few months later. I don't think that the U.S. steel industry got any more efficient or benefited substantially from these artificial protections. A few years later, the U.S. steel industry continues to decline in size as production from India and China has grown tremendously. If you invested in these steel companies, you might have made money when the protections were put in place but you would likely have lost it when they were eventually removed.

Tariffs and embargoes have a long and sordid history. The Smoot-Hawley Act of 1930 imposed fixed-dollar tariffs on imports into the United States of a wide variety of items and had the dual effect of ruining relations with our biggest trading partner (Canada) and likely worsening the economic depression in the United States. Trade embargoes (when a country is forbidden to trade with another) are also of dubious value, as they tend to hurt everyone involved, and people go to tremendous effort to find ways (legal or illegal) around them.

The Bell Tolls for Toll Roads

You should also be careful with investments in situations where the livelihood of the company depends on the government allowing agreed-upon rate increases to go into effect. These types of situations develop in a number of industries such as utilities, telecom, and toll roads/transportation projects. In the latter case, the government typically grants the right to a certain company to build and operate a toll road for a certain amount of time (20 to 30 years), with the right to collect tolls over that period providing the return on their investment. The agreements generally include a schedule of tariff increases throughout the life of the contract.

This is where the trouble comes in. In a few years, the road is operating smoothly. The ribbon-cutting ceremony has faded in people's memories and suddenly the scheduled rate increase comes up. The poor consumers (voters, in many cases) complain loudly that life is terribly hard for them in some way and that the corporate fat cats should not get rich at their expense. Conveniently forgetting that the road would not have been built without the corporate fat cats, the politicians quickly take the side of these consumers and find a way to delay or put off altogether the toll increase. The company that put the money up to build the toll road (or subway or electricity grid or whatever) and its shareholders get the short end of the stick. There may be a lengthy court battle, but most likely there will be some sort of compromise, which, by definition, takes something away from the company and its shareholders, reducing the value of their investment.

The Politics of International Investing

Political will can be very fickle, so I would never choose to invest in something that relies on political will. Often politicians choose to blame the mistakes of the past for their current problems. Remember that they are also trying to gain as much popular support as possible, whether for votes or simply to be popular. When push comes to shove, it is usually what is going to gain the most political brownie points that wins out. Sometimes governments surprise us and do something that is unpopular but necessary.

In one recent example of this, there was a potentially very unpopular doubling of consumer fuel prices in Indonesia. Indonesia was well known in Asia for its government's subsidy of oil prices, which kept consumers (and voters) happy by keeping prices low at the pump, but had the unhappy side consequence of driving an ever higher budget deficit as the government continued to spend to subsidize the cost of oil. As oil prices climbed to $60 per barrel and beyond in 2004 and 2005, it became clear that the government could not maintain these subsidies because of the increasingly negative impact on their budget situation. What happened next is telling. The Indonesian currency declined in value because international investors lost faith in the Indonesian government's ability to keep financing this subsidy. To its credit, the elected government took the difficult decision to start moving toward a market price for fuel. The first step toward that, on October 1, 2005, had the effect of nearly doubling the cost of gas at the pump in Indonesia. Just by coincidence, that same week, two bombs went off in the resort island of Bali. You might think that the impact of these two dramatic developments on consumer sentiment and business outlook would have sent the stock market down. Interestingly, investors recognized that the government was doing what needed to be done and that the bombing, while tragic, was an isolated incident. The local stock market went up in the days following, and the currency got stronger.

This chapter discussed the role of government protections through tariffs and the granting of monopolies in business. It also presented instances where the market corrected these artificial barriers through trade and technology.

My advice: Avoid these situations from the very beginning. Whenever somebody (be extra cautious if the person is an investment banker or a stockbroker) tells you that a company is protected by some law or long-term agreement, move on to the next story. Political will is usually very short term. You are better off making investments in situations where the free market and the abilities of that company and management are put to the test and rewarded. That is where your stock-picking abilities will be appropriately tested, and where you are more likely to make money.

Chapter SEVEN

Know the Shareholders

Always know who is on your team. You should make sure that you know who is behind any company that you are investing in. You should find out who the management is, what their track record is, and how well management gets along with the government or regulator. This is important because you don't want to be surprised by something related to management or fraud.

What Can Destroy a Company Virtually Overnight?

If something starts to go wrong with a company's business, it's unlikely that the business would deteriorate so quickly and dramatically that a stock would fall more than 10 or 20 percent suddenly. What can cause a stock to fall suddenly and shockingly is management fraud or

155

some decision or change that dramatically alters the business. The emergence of a new competitor or a new product, a dropoff in sales, or the failure of some new business venture is unlikely to materialize overnight. Most companies release at least a couple of updates per year on how their business is going. In many cases you get quarterly updates, so you know what is happening every three months.

A careful reading of the press releases that the company puts out to accompany their financial results and a quick review of the numbers themselves will tell you a lot about the status of a company. Details about the revenue are what usually tell you whether the company is calling for price increases or price decreases and also whether the company is selling more of a product (increasing in volume). Has revenue increased from the previous year? Are there any increases from the preceding quarter? Is there seasonal impact? And on the expense side, are costs as a percentage of revenues increasing? Decreasing margins in a business that is growing are a red flag as well. Is this a company that is appropriately investing in its future? Or one that cannot control its costs? If you start to see disturbing trends in the business results of an investment, you should look for a more detailed understanding of what's going wrong. However, it's very unlikely that a company would suffer a fatal blow overnight, in just three months, or even in six months. Suffice it to say that almost every corporate disaster has given investors plenty of warning and plenty of time to get out. The exception is when management fraud or some change external to the company brings it all crashing down. *This* can happen overnight.

External shocks that can impact a company very dramatically and suddenly include court cases, changes in government policy, or certain disastrous acts of God that have a severe effect on the operation of the company. Companies need to declare in their filings with the SEC the existence of potential impact of any significant court cases. That's not to say that a company's claims that it expects to prevail in a court case will always come true, but investors should at least know the risks that are out there.

Consider a pharmaceutical company that is facing a challenge to one of its patents. As a major drug approaches the end of its patent life, the pharmaceutical company will often file for additional patent protection. The company devises some slight variation on the drug in question in an attempt to continue to generate revenues and profits from the flagging sales. Other companies in the same industry will charge that a game is being played, that a slight tweak to a drug to buy the company more years of patent protection is just a ruse.

In a real-life instance of this, an Indian drug company sued the makers of Lipitor in U.S. federal court. Lipitor is one of Pfizer's major drugs, for which the patent will expire in the next few years. A court decision against Pfizer would have had a sudden and dramatic impact on it's stock price. This was a risk that Pfizer investors needed to consider when assessing the value and potential reward of an investment there. In the end, the Indian company lost the case and Pfizer shares rose.

A change in government policy can have a dramatic impact on a company as well. There are plenty of other government moves in terms of tax policy and benefits, sales restrictions, and other issues that can bounce back to the company. Remember that in many economies and societies, government plays a stronger role in determining the fortunes of a company than we're used to in the United States.

The risk of some external shock or government impact on a business or industry is not unique to the international markets. While there have been some high-profile examples of the nationalization of a particular business or industry, such as the nationalization of the oil industry in Venezuela in 1976 and the nationalization of the Suez canal in Egypt in 1956, these are more rare than people think. Most governments around the world now recognize that predictable policies and reliable regulations make for a positive investment environment. The attraction of international money to help build the infrastructure and business environment in a country is good for the government and for the country, the business community, and the population. And as I've explained, proper diversification across a variety of companies and industries can help reduce—or at least control—the risk of some outlandish move by a government.

One of the key things investors can do to protect

themselves in any sort of investment is to know the stakeholders. You have to know who you're investing with, as well as knowing what you're investing in.

How Does My Business, Industry, and Management Relate to the Government?

Just as financial statements can give investors warnings about how a business is going, governments, through their actions and statements, warn of their intentions with regard to a company management team or industry. Chapter 5 explained the importance of aligning investments with government preferences, policies, and priorities.

A Notorious Example: Yukos

Significant moves by a government to take over a company or industry are very rare. Even in one of the most notorious examples, when the Russian government essentially stole oil and gas company Yukos from the public shareholders in broad daylight, there were warning signs well before that happened. This is a useful case study, demonstrating the types of warnings and the opportunities for shareholders to get out of the way of such a freight train. But first, some history is in order.

Just after the collapse of the Soviet Union in the early 1990s, observers looking at the Russian oil industry would have seen hundreds of stand-alone, state-owned

entities focused in one particular section of the industry or one part of the country. As with much of the
old Soviet-era industry, many of these companies were
overstaffed, unprofitable, and inefficiently run. One of
Russia's largest oil producers and a major refining and
petrochemical company were combined to form Yukos.
The company also gained control over a number of
distribution companies. At this point, Yukos remained
entirely state-owned. By the end of 1995, problems with
state ownership were evident. The company was in
technical bankruptcy, and its debts to the government
were $3.5 billion. Through a series of auctions in 1995
and 1996, Yukos became Russia's first fully privatized
oil company.

A new management team, under the leadership of
bank executive Mikhail Khodorkovsky, took over in early
1996. Heavy investment during 1996 and 1997 led to
increased production capacity and improving financial
fortunes. The company made a series of acquisitions in
1997 and 1998 and soon became a significant global
player in oil and gas. In 1999 and 2000, the company
started making moves to consolidate its ownership in
subsidiaries as part of a corporate restructuring that
included the issuance of an ADR in New York in 2001.

By 2003, however, things took a turn for the worse.
That summer, Khodorkovsky's business partner was
arrested and accused of theft of state property in connection with the 1994 privatization of a fertilizer plant. That
arrest was widely seen as a warning to Khodorkovsky,

who at the time was financing and supporting the liberal opposition to the leadership of conservative president Vladimir Putin.

In July 2003, Yukos shares traded at $45. Anyone familiar with the rest of the story will realize that was a pretty good time to sell. In a series of court battles related to tax payments over the next couple of years, Yukos management lost control of the company. It was finally sold off at a fire-sale price to a shadowy group in early 2005. As of late 2005, Yukos shares traded at just $7. Khodorkovsky took a steep fall from grace. His wealth was frozen by the government and he was sentenced to six years in jail for fraud at the eerily named YaG 14/10 penal colony in Siberia.

As I see it, the moral of the Yukos story is that you should be on the lookout for warning signs that something is going wrong. The arrest of the business partner was widely reported in the summer of 2003, and any investor should have realized that nothing good comes from an executive being thrown in jail. When was the last time you heard of a business that improved after the government arrested someone from the company's management? That's not to say that everyone who is arrested is guilty, but as an investor, you don't have to go along for the ride. At a minimum, you are looking at months, quarters, or years of uncertainty and lack of strategic direction, not to mention the tremendous legal bills that go along with any lawsuit.

Other examples of warnings of problems ahead

include the early signs that Parmalat was in trouble and the press reports that presaged the complete collapse of Enron. In the case of Parmalat, astute investors would have been able to protect most of their investment if they had sold out in February 2003 when Parmalat pulled a €500 million bond issue from the market or in March of that year when the CFO resigned. The company went into administration (bankruptcy) in December and the equity was worthless at that point. Also in the case of Enron, the shares were still trading at $26 in mid-October when articles in the *Wall Street Journal* began raising questions about their finances. By the end of November, the shares were below $1.

My advice is: "Run, don't walk" from situations like this.

Chapter EIGHT

Buy the Banks

If you think about it, all business activity is somehow tied to a bank. Somewhere along the line, money was either borrowed from a bank, banking services were used and fees paid, or, at least, the profits (hopefully) were deposited into a bank. In running my business I have been shocked at the fees that the bank collects from me—and they have the audacity to clear checks out of my account instantly but still take their sweet time before crediting my account for checks that I have deposited. As you can imagine, the banks collect fees or interest along the way and can become a good play on growth in a particular country. Furthermore, many banks are publicly listed, giving us lots of different opportunities to invest in the sector.

Of course, there have been a number of spectacular banking system failures in recent history (Latin America,

Southeast Asia, . . .). However, such banking crises are often the best thing to happen to investors—Not for the investors who held bank shares at the time, but as a way of purging a sector of bad companies and bad loans and providing solid growth for the future. In fact, over time, banking stocks have provided investors with attractive returns relative to other sectors.

Because of their need for capital and their attractiveness as an investment vehicle, many banks worldwide are listed. In fact, financial stocks make up nearly 15 percent of the total ADRs in the U.S. markets, making them one of the larger industries represented. See Figures 8.1 and 8.2.

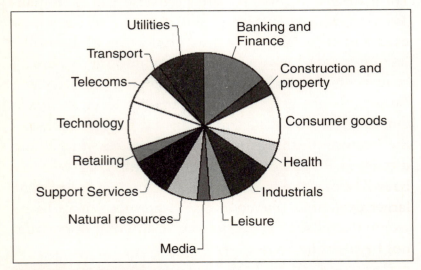

Figure 8.1   ADRs by Sector
(Source: Bank of New York)

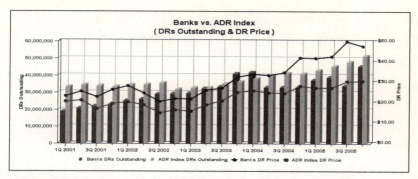

Figure 8.2 Performance of Largest Banks Relative to Global Markets as a Whole
(Source: Bank of New York)

Banking Meltdowns

For a variety of reasons, banks are susceptible to many forms of risk and the occasional crisis or meltdown. One of the risks that banks face is *liquidity risk*. This is also known as a "run on a bank," when many depositors request withdrawals of their money at the same time. Because banks are in the business of taking customer deposits and then lending them to other customers that are businesses, the banks clearly don't keep all of the money on hand for customers to show up and demand back. Unfortunately, a run on a bank is typically tied to larger economic problems, which may make depositors worry that if they're not first in line, their money may not be there when they get to the bank. As a result, the performance of banks and bank shares can magnify underlying problems in an economy or a market.

165

Another risk that banks face is *credit risk*. This is the risk that people who owe money to the bank won't repay. This too is exacerbated in an economic crisis, which can contribute to extreme volatility in bank shares and bank performance.

The final type of bank risk is *interest-rate risk*, where the interest-rate environment develops in such a way that the bank has to pay more for deposits than they earn on loans.

Discussion of these risks is not intended to scare you off investing in banks. All businesses involve risks. In fact, although things can go very badly for banks during a period of economic trouble, the rewards can outweigh the risks when properly managed. While working on this book, I spent some time getting to know the Japanese banking sector and following its performance. Bank shares in Japan performed tremendously in 2005 and 2006 as investors used banks as a way to play a recovery in Japan.

Prominent examples of things going wrong include the savings-and-loan industry in the United States in the 1980s and early 1990s, the banking crisis in Japan during the 1990s along with the debt defaults by debtor countries in Latin America in the 1980s.

In the 1980s, mismanagement, interest rates, spectacular speculation, and trouble in the real estate market caused a wave of failures of savings-and-loan institutions that eventually cost the U.S. government and taxpayers

$125 billion. In addition to mismanagement and, in some cases, outright fraud, the savings and loans suffered from interest-rate risk. Many depositors were moving to newly created higher-interest money market funds when the S&Ls were largely stuck in long-term mortgages, which, with interest rates rising, were falling in value. The recently deregulated S&Ls entered into riskier and riskier ventures to try to close the gap.

As a result of the S&L crisis, regulations were tightened and the regulators themselves got better at identifying mismanagement and combating fraud. The banking system in the United States today is quite healthy, is carefully monitored, and is a source of some very good investment opportunities. As this chapter explains, the opportunities for investment in the banking sector typically improve after a crisis.

The banking crisis in Japan in the 1990s had its roots in the boom years of the late 1980s. At that time, soaring property values and share prices provided collateral for huge bank loans throughout the economy. When the property market and stock market crashed, the virtuous circle of borrowing fueling asset price inflation fueling further investment, and so on, came to a sudden stop.

As a result of the crisis in Japan, four mega–banking groups emerged to dominate banking in Japan. These new groups are better able to handle bad loans and absorb smaller players that find themselves in trouble. In addition, Japan's bank watchdog—the Financial Supervisory Agency—forced the banks to be more transparent and report more regularly on the condition and value of their portfolios.

Many of the Japanese banks provided tremendous gains for investors in 2005. Some of the larger banks were up 50 percent or more. This is a spectacular return for companies of this size.

The boom and bust of the economies and banking systems of Southeast Asia in the 1990s followed a pattern similar to that in Japan. The economy of Thailand, for example, had a compound average growth rate of 10 percent from 1985 through 1995. The joke at the time was that the overhead cranes that were ubiquitous on the Bangkok skyline were the national bird of Thailand. Buildings seemed to appear overnight, with gleaming multistory structures replacing the traditional houses throughout much of the city. Along with development came wealth. The banks had more money than they knew what to do with and were lending it to anyone they could find. Of course, this involved lending to many unattractive businesses and receiving bad debt and low returns in exchange. In July 1997, the Thai baht, which had been at 25 to the U.S. dollar for 13 years, was suddenly allowed to float. It immediately halved in value. Chapter 9 discusses the currency market and how this came to pass, but suffice it to say that it was devastating to the Thai economy and to the banking system.

Banks 101: Peculiarities of Investing in Banks

Banks are a useful play on business activity because they provide the fuel that allows companies to grow faster than their internally generated funds would allow them to grow without diluting the existing shareholders by issuing more shares.

Banks get money from depositors, keep some of it in reserve, and lend the rest out to businesses and individuals. The amount that has to be kept in reserve is set by the government. This provides governments with an important lever to control economic activity. If they are trying to slow economic growth, they can raise the amount that has to be kept in reserve, making less available to lend out. Conversely, if they want to encourage growth, they can lower the requirement, which will likely boost lending.

There are a few terms and concepts you should know when you are considering investing in banks.

Capital requirements: Usually set by the market regulator, capital requirements are typically the amount of cash and equivalents (i.e., government bonds) that a bank must maintain for its normal operations. This is often discussed as a *reserve ratio* (a percentage of deposits). Customer confidence that there are adequate reserves is crucial to prevent crippling runs on banks, when all of the customers show up at once to claim their funds.

169

Net interest margin: This is a major measure of the banks' ability to make money on their loans and is calculated as interest earned on loans minus interest paid on deposits. This is the gross margin for financial institutions and is sometimes referred to as the *spread.*

Nonperforming loans: This is the group of loans on which interest is not being paid. They are also known as *bad loans.*

The following are risks to watch out for:

- *Scandals* (the temptation of too much money lying around). As bank robber Willie Sutton is famously quoted as saying, he robbed banks because "that's where they keep the money." The lure of money lying around has proven to be too much for bank executives from Arizona (home of the U.S. savings-and-loan scandal in the 1980s) to the Vatican (where $70 million in missing funds is still under investigation).

- *Bad lending policies* (corruption and the influence of politics). One of the major risks of banks is that their loans will not get paid back. While there are loan loss reserves set aside to deal with this eventuality, they are often not sufficient. Bank officials are sometimes swayed by political concerns such that corporations owned by family members or friends of the ruling political elite get preferential

treatment and receive loans that would not otherwise be made. The loans often turn into de facto
gifts to the powerful people, since they are never
paid back.

Here are a few suggestions to avoid the pitfalls of
investing in banks in international markets:

- *Invest in countries where there has already been a
  banking scandal.* Large banking scandals typically
  lead to accusations of lax regulation. In places like
  this, regulation is often tightened significantly in
  the wake of a scandal. In Asia, for example, the
  weaknesses in the system exposed by the currency,
  banking, and economic crisis of the late 1990s
  encouraged governments to tighten reserve requirements, accelerate bankruptcy procedures, and keep
  a more careful eye on what their banks were doing.
  Investing in a bank after a crisis can involve less risk
  than before.

- *Understand where the banking industry in a particular country is, relative to certain industry standards,
  such as the Basel Accords.* The Basel Accords are
  global standardized bank regulations agreed to by a
  committee established by the G10 countries (Western Europe, Japan, and North America) and being
  encouraged for adoption by other countries as well.
  These accords standardize the measurement of risk
  and available capital. As a country moves toward

adoption of the Basel Accords, the weakest banks will not make it and the strong ones need to get stronger still. I believe that if investors are aware of where a banking system stands in relation to the process of strengthening and increasing regulation, they can make better decisions about investing in the banking sector.

- *Diversfy among a few banks in a market or (even better) banks in a few markets.* While banks are great plays on economic growth and business activity, they, like all companies, can have company-specific issues. Issues such as bad management, high loan concentration in a particular industry, and fraud, can make a particular bank a bad investment. To minimize company-risk, investors should buy shares in a few banks in a particular market or, even better, a few banks in each of a few markets.

Overall, the banking sector can be a great way to invest in the health and growth in an economy. The sector can serve as a proxy for overall economic growth and in many cases provides above average returns and profits.

Chapter NINE

The Impact of Currency

F oreign exchange is nowhere near as complicated as people assume. It is a fundamental concept that shouldn't intimidate individual investors. In fact, understanding a few simple rules regarding currency should be enough to give you the opportunity to consider exchange rates when you're making your international investments.

The most likely place you'll encounter the impact of foreign exchange most directly is when traveling to another country. Before setting off to vacation in Mexico, for example, an American might convert $100 into Mexican pesos. At the current exchange rate, you, as a traveler, would receive just over a thousand pesos for your hundred dollars. On your trip, you might use those 1,056 pesos to buy food or products, pay a taxi driver, or the like. A year ago, that same $100 would have gotten you

1,124 pesos. On last year's vacation you might have been able to spend those extra 68 pesos on an additional post-card or souvenir. This year it is slightly more expensive for you to take a trip to Mexico. For some reason, the market has decided that the Mexican peso is more valuable and that the U.S. dollar is less valuable than they were 12 months ago. The U.S. traveler gets fewer pesos for $100.

What changed over the past 12 months? Perhaps people's expectations of the outlook for the Mexican economy have improved. Perhaps their view of the U.S. economy has become more pessimistic. A variety of different factors could lead the market to decide that pesos were more valuable and U.S. dollars less valuable over the past 12 months. Higher interest rates in Mexico relative to the United States, for example, may have attracted investment there. Improved political stability in Mexico may also have led to the strength. In any case, it is important to remember that the fluctuations of a country's currency are simply a matter of supply and demand.

The supply side of the equation is determined largely by the governments themselves. Governments are mostly free to do as they see fit. Governments (actually the central banks in most countries) carefully watch economic activity to determine the appropriate amount of money to provide (the money supply). Too much money can lead to inflation and too little can slow economic growth and cause an increase in unemployment.

This chapter explains the supply and demand of currency and its impact on foreign exchange rates, as well as the connection between strong economies and strong currencies. It also shows how the U.S. dollar–denominated investments benefit from stronger currencies overseas relative to the U.S. dollar.

Rule 1: Money Is Like Any Other Product—Its Value Fluctuates with Demand and Supply

If more people worldwide want more coffee, its value will rise and the price will go up. If fewer people want coffee, prices will fall. If there is a bumper crop of coffee and the supply grows tremendously, outpacing demand, prices will fall. The same is true of currency. If people want to own U.S. dollars, the price will rise. If the U.S. government decides to print more money and supply begins to outstrip demand, the value (price) of a dollar will fall.

To illustrate how the demand side of the equation might work in a fictional example, let's imagine a country called Newcountry (Newco) and another called Oldcountry (Oldco). Newco has a strong, stable government and a growing economy. Suddenly one fine January morning, some army generals in Newco decide things would be better (for them, probably) if they ran the country. They stage a coup and take over the government. Trading partners of theirs, such as those in Oldco, dislike this dramatic change in Newco and as a result of the higher level of uncertainty, they decide to withdraw some of their investments from Newco. This leads to a decline in demand for Newco's currency, which causes its price/value to fall. The impact of political uncertainty on the country's currency can be dramatic. Investors will always demand an appropriate valuation for any investment that they have, including whether they have to factor in the impact of uncertainty, volatility, and change. It is likely that they'll demand a higher return and therefore offer a lower price. Just as you would demand a higher return to offset the risk associated with investing in a very new biotech company compared with an old, stable company like IBM, Coca-Cola, or Disney, international investors demand a higher return to offset the uncertainty when governments and politicians give them reason to doubt, or least be concerned about, the future direction of a government or country. Part of the way that investors get that higher return to offset the higher risk is through currency and exchange rates.

Rule 2: Strong Economies Usually Provide Stronger Currencies

Back to our Newco/Oldco example. Imagine that Newco has had a strong economy with economic growth of 10 percent in each of the last three years. Oldco has not been doing as well, as its economy has been growing at only 2 percent for each of the last three years. It is likely that money will be in great demand in Newco. As businesses are expanding, building new buildings, hiring more people, and making more products, they have to borrow money from the banks and from investors, driving up the value of money in Newco.

Within a country's borders, the value of money is reflected by the interest rate. The interest rate is truly the cost of money. As years of economic growth continue, it is likely that the interest rate will climb from, say, 8 percent to 12 percent. All that economic growth needs to be funded somehow, and businesses find themselves competing with each other to borrow the money from the banks to expand in the growing economy.

Contrast that with the situation in Oldco, whose measly 2 percent growth rate likely has not demanded much in the way of business expansion or business investment. As a result, money is not a hot commodity in Oldco. Businesses there aren't expanding, aren't building new buildings, aren't making more products, and therefore they're not creating demand for money. If there aren't good investment opportunities, businesses will not demand money, and interest rates will remain flat or decline. Perhaps in Oldco over the past three years, interest rates have fallen from 8 percent to 5 percent. So what should investors in Oldco do? Should they put their money in a bank in Oldco and earn 5 percent? What if they could put it in a bank in Newco and earn 12 percent?

It's likely that quite a lot of money is flowing from the slow-growing Oldco into the fast-growing Newco, and every time that money moves into a new economy, demand for the currency in that economy grows.

Remember: Exchange rates are simply a reflection of demand and supply for money. In this case, because of the higher level of economic growth that resulted in higher interest rates in Newco, it is likely that money is flowing into Newco and the demand for Newco currency is growing. As a result, the value of the Newco currency is going to be rising. This is a very simplistic example that ignores the potential for government intervention, the likelihood of differing political environments and investment climates, and other changes in terms of productivity, resources, and so on, but it does serve to show that stronger economies usually lead to stronger currencies and weaker economies usually lead to weaker currencies.

As you think about where to invest your hard-earned dollars around the world, you're likely to find better opportunities in strong economies than in weak ones. Strong economies tend to be the tide that lifts all boats, which means investment opportunities improve as well. It is not hard to understand that a business has an easier time generating growth, sales, and profits in a growing economy than in a shrinking or stagnant one. In this way, we, as investors, are fortunate. It's likely that the places in which we're finding attractive investments are also the places where currencies are strengthening and improving our investment return. Things are, of course, a little more complicated—because we're buying U.S. dollar–denominated investments in companies that are showing their revenues and that make their profits in their local currency. This requires one last rule.

Rule 3: U.S. Dollar–Denominated Investments Benefit from Other Currencies Being Stronger Than the Dollar

What if I, as a U.S. investor, were investing in stocks in companies in Newco? What would be the impact of currency changes on my investment? There are a few things to take into consideration. First, what is the performance of my home economy/currency (the United States/U.S. dollar) relative to that of Newco? Using the preceding fictional example of three years of growth at 10 percent, it's clear that Newco is growing faster than the U.S. economy. As investors like myself look for investment opportunities in Newco, we're creating demand for Newco's currency and driving up its value. At the same time, we're selling U.S. dollars to make those investments in the Newco currency.

Remember our example from the beginning of this chapter of you as the intrepid U.S. traveler who went to Mexico? When you bought your thousand pesos, you sold a hundred U.S. dollars. In a minor way, you created more demand for pesos and less demand for dollars. You sold your dollars for pesos. I'm doing the same thing by taking my U.S. dollars and investing them in Newco. I'm taking a small amount of my money and creating more demand for Newco's currency. In this situation of buying locally listed shares of foreign companies, there is an intermediate step. My investment is still in my local currency (U.S. dollars), so as more investors like myself invest in Newco businesses and opportunities, and the value of Newco's currency rises (while, let's assume, the U.S. currency remains the same), the relative value of Newco's currency to the U.S. dollar rises. Because my Newco company makes its sales and earns its profits in Newco currency but my investment is priced in U.S. dollars, I benefit from this trend.

Returning to a real-world example, imagine that I own one ADR, which represents one share of a Japanese bank. When I make my investment, the bank is trading at ¥1,000 per share in Japan, which translates to U.S. $10, as the exchange rate sits at ¥100 per U.S. dollar. Say the bank earns profits of ¥100 per share, which translates into U.S. $1. So my $10 ADR is trading at 10 times the U.S. dollar Earnings Per Share (EPS) of one dollar. Say that over the next couple of years the Japanese economy grows faster than the U.S. economy, which changes the exchange rate such that that same ¥100 is now worth U.S. $1.25. It now takes more U.S. dollars to buy ¥100. In fact, it would take $12.50 to buy ¥1,000 share. So, all things being equal, if someone wanted to buy my thousand-yen share in my Japanese bank, they have to give me $12.50 for it rather than the $10 I paid.

Looked at another way, my stock just got cheaper. Say my share price remained unchanged at $10. My shares used to trade at a P/E ratio of 10 times when ¥100 equaled U.S. $1. Now my $10 stock has an EPS of $1.25 rather than $1. As a result, the P/E ratio falls from 10 times to 8 times. Chances are, that stock price will not remain unchanged. It would likely rise to keep the P/E at 10 times, and the shares would move up to $12.50. So I can either keep my now magically cheaper share or sell it for 25 percent more than what I bought it for. Clearly this is a very simple example, but it does serve to illustrate that when we are investing in strong economies and buying the U.S. dollar version of foreign investments, we can benefit not only from the rise in the price of the share but also from the rising value of the currency that the underlying investment works in.

The recent performance of Brazilian investments provides a good example of this. In 2005, the São Paulo index (the BOVESPA) rose by about 28 percent (from 26,196 to 33,456). So if you had bought one unit of the index, your investment would have risen by nearly 30 percent over the year. However, if you used U.S. dollars to make that investment and were considering the value of it in U.S. dollars at the end of the period, you would have done even better. At the beginning of the year, U.S. $1 bought 2.65 Brazilian Reals. By the end, however, that same U.S. dollar bought only 2.33 Brazilian Reals, because of improved sentiment about the direction and health of the Brazilian economy. The currency strengthened by 14 percent, so if you invested U.S. $100 at the beginning of the year in a local Brazilian index, the strength of the index alone would have made

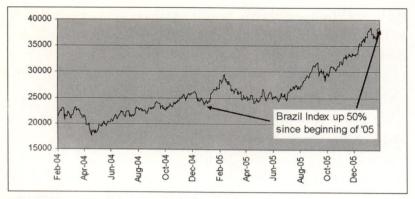

Figure 9.1   Brazilian Index Return 2005

that $100 investment worth $128. But in reality you are converting dollars into Brazilian currency to make your investment and then converting those Brazilian Reals back into U.S. dollars when you sell your investment. Your investment actually went from $100 to $128 as a result of the index strength, but the strength of the currency appreciation added another 14 percent to your

Figure 9.2   Brazilian Currency Performance 2005

return. When you went to sell your investment and con-
verted back into U.S. dollars, you would actually get
$146. As a result, the strength in the Brazilian economy
was reflected both in the stock index and in the strength
of the currency, and your investment would have
returned nearly 50 percent over one year. See Figures 9.1
and 9.2.

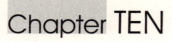

Chapter TEN

Don't Be the Last One In

Investors need to be careful about being the last one into a stock, market, idea or trend. The old phrase "the last one in is a rotten egg" applies very much in investing.

One of the most disturbing afflictions you will see among investors is greed, especially when it makes them forget the fundamentals of what they're doing. Greed makes some people blind to the risks they are taking. If a market has already gone up a lot, it has the potential to go down a lot. Certainly you should participate in strong upward moves in a market, but you need to know when a market has already gone up too much. If you see that a market is up 30 or 40 percent in a year, chances are it is ready for a correction or at least the chances are higher that a correction might take place. Investors are better served by finding areas where other people are not yet looking. Finding the hotspots is not finding spots that are hot right now (or have been hot for a while), it is finding the spots that are about to be hot. By applying the lessons explained in this book, you should be able to find attractive opportunities that are reasonably valued rather than participating in momentum that is just about to crack.

In the late 1990s, everyone in America was making a mint investing in Internet stocks—except for the professional investors. Many fund managers and mutual fund companies did not participate in the strong growth in Internet stocks in the late 1990s because they were applying a discipline that they had learned over many years and over many boom and bust cycles in the market. These fund managers were battered year after year after year as retail investors invested more and more in high-flying stocks like Pets.com and Amazon.com. Pretty soon, individual investors had convinced themselves that they didn't need the professionals anymore, and they were pulling their money out of the mutual funds in droves. This, of course, drove the fund managers completely crazy, and at the end of 1999, they finally threw up their hands and started putting their money into the high-flying tech stocks. In the three months between January 1, 2000, and the break in the market that began April 8, the NASDAQ was up 27% percent before peaking at 5050. Of course, the rest of the story is history. The NASDAQ began correcting, and correcting dramatically. It took not only retail investors with it but the fund managers who had finally capitulated and participated in the final top of the market.

Separating good performance from momentum is difficult, if not impossible. First, just look at the percentages. If something is up 30 or 40 percent, chances are that the fundamentals of that company or that market haven't changed by 30 or 40 percent. The world simply doesn't get 30 or 40 percent better in only a few short months.

As I write this in early 2006, the India market is up more than 28% year to date. Of course, this corrects a longstanding weakness in the Indian stock market whereby investors frustrated with the slow pace of reform and growth in India and simply stopped investing in the market. That underperformance, however, is more than resolved. The market now trades just south of 20 P/E. Twenty-two times P/E is all well and good for a particular company, but it's not applicable for the entire market. Think about the rules you would apply if you were buying into a company. You would want to buy at a P/E somewhat close to its growth rate. Often investors will look at a company's earnings growth—say, 10 percent, 15 percent, or 18 percent—and imagine that a P/E equal to that growth rate is the appropriate price to pay. Remember, one of the major schools of thought in investing is that of growth at a reasonable price (GARP). Sure, you want growth, but you want to pay a reasonable price for it. Applying the same rule to the country of India as a whole means that we're expecting the growth rate of the country or the average growth rate of all the companies in that country to be about 20 percent. This would be an unprecedented growth rate. Countries showing growth of 8 or 9 percent are rare enough; 20 percent is simply unheard of. I would much rather buy into India after it has adjusted a bit or after some earnings growth has made the valuations a bit more reasonable. There are certainly good companies in India, but as a whole, the market itself looks quite expensive.

Another good example of a market that has me a little bit worried is the market for Shanghai real estate. Pick up any copy of a recent magazine that talks about the rate of development in China and there is likely to be an article about how much Shanghai has grown in recent years.

Perhaps I'm a bit conservative, but I would rather have a number of different opportunities working for me than have all of my bets on one big opportunity, especially in an investment that perhaps is up 20 or 30 percent already.

Road Signs—When to Pull Over

As I already said, I would want to be careful investing into a market that is already up 30 percent. If you start seeing a market that's gone up that much start to decline it can be a pretty scary thing. It can be hard to get out of stocks. And even good stocks will go down quite dramatically.

It's easy to say "sell at the top" or "don't buy before a market is about to crash," but how do you know?

I have three rules for deciding when to sell, which I refer to as "road signs," employing a driving analogy.

1. Look in your rearview mirror.

2. Look at what you are driving.

3. Look down the road ahead of you.

Look in Your Rearview Mirror

To have some idea of where you're going, it's important to know where you've been. Looking in the rearview mirror is another way of saying that you've got to know where you've come from.

Luckily, financial markets are measured in numbers, so it's easy to see where you've come from. You can find out how much a market has changed in recent months. Information is widely available—we hear nearly every day how much the Dow Jones or the S&P 500 is up year to date, in the past month or over the past year. That same information is available about indexes around the world if you know where to look.

It's not hard to look around the world and find out how markets have been doing relative to each other. You can find it on any financial web site—for example, www.yahoo.com, www.bloomberg.com, or www.bnyadr.com. These sites show you the performance over the past one month and three months, and for the year to date, which is a good place to start in terms of assessing which markets are up too much already and which have further to go.

Look at What You're Driving

Is what you're driving the most expensive car on the road? Is it the fanciest thing you've seen for miles? Perhaps that raises your risk a little bit. Look at the P/E of the stocks that you own relative to the market. Are they at about the market average? Is there a reason that they should be trading higher than the average company in that market? Chances are you'll answer yes to that question. After all, you own the stock. You bought it because you believed in it. Owning a stock with a PE multiple of 40 in a market that trades at 15 times on average can be right in some situations, but it always involves a higher level of risk than owning a stock with a lower valuation. Be sure you know what you're driving and where the brakes are.

Look Down the Road Ahead of You

Has anything changed? Is there anything that's different about the world since you developed your theme? Are oil prices higher? Has international trade changed? What about political tensions? If you own a computer stock in the United States and you believe the business community is holding back from buying new computers because a new operating system is expected to come out, then take that into consideration. You don't have to be a high-tech expert to recognize such changes. Owning stocks anywhere is just a matter paying attention. Paying attention gives you an advantage over everyone else because the information about the future is often being reported in the present. It might take some digging, but

Think Like a Local

Look carefully at how the markets have performed. It's a very important to understand what you're looking at, however. Many statistics actually reflect the performance of that market in terms of U.S. dollars. While that may be important to the investor's bottom line, but it's not necessarily helpful. The U.S. dollar performance of a stock market combines the performance of the stock index itself with the performance of the currency. Without getting too technical, what we're really concerned about when we want to gauge relative performance is how well the market has done in terms of the local currency. A Brazilian investor doesn't know and probably doesn't care what the U.S. dollar performance of an index has been. When was the last time you considered the performance of the Dow in Japanese yen? As the majority of investment decisions in the local market are being made by locals, think about it from their perspective: If the index has gone from 100 to 110, then it's only a 10 percent increase. If, in addition, the currency strengthened by 10 percent relative to the U.S. dollar, then the U.S. dollar return would be 20 percent. Now relative to some other markets and your general feeling for momentum in the market, 20 percent might be too much. However, you should be thinking about the situation in terms of the local currency.

the information is almost always there. So always look down the road ahead, and don't blind yourself to information that disagrees with your own point of view. Also remember to not be too optimistic. If you think there's light at the end of the tunnel, consider that it might be a train coming at you.

Of course, you don't just want to buy the worst-performing markets and you shouldn't just blindly buy something that has underperformed other markets. That's not the point of this discussion at all. The point is that you should assess the risk of another downturn in a market, which could happen as quickly as or even more quickly than an upturn.

Conclusion

This book has endeavored to provide tools and structures to help you make decisions about international
investments related to specific themes, enabling you
to identify and play themes that you believe in or aspects
of your life that you think could provide good investment opportunities. To ensure adequate shelf life for
this book, I've tried to avoid providing specific ideas for
investments, but rather I've focused on providing examples that demonstrate how to build your own themes
and ideas. However, this conclusion provides me with
the opportunity to offer my two cents about investment
themes that I think will be applicable for 2006, 2007,
and beyond. Please bear in mind that different people's
portfolios, appetites for risk, and investment goals might
make some of these investments either appropriate or
inappropriate for you in particular. These are simply

my thoughts and might not be relevant to your investment goals.

Demographics

One of the most impressive aspects of international investment is the ability to play demographic trends. Here in the United States, the aging of the population has led many people to invest in stocks related to pharmaceuticals, home health care, travel and leisure, and other themes that are connected to this demographic factor. Internationally there are likewise some countries that are experiencing a significant aging of the population, such as Japan and Germany. Many of the themes being used in the U.S. market to play the demographic trends here would be similarly applicable in those markets. As the older populations in these countries grow, the demand proportionately increases for leisure services to occupy their increased free time and for pharmaceutical and health services to address the changing needs of their aging bodies. Outperformance of these sectors and, certainly, the opportunity to identify winners in related industries provide many possible investment themes. Far more interesting to me, however, are those countries where a significant portion of the population is young and just entering their peak earning, consuming, and investing years. I recently returned from a trip to Mexico City. Of the hundred million people in Mexico today, 77 percent of them are under the age of

39. As this population bulge moves through the years, expect homebuilders, auto sellers, retailers, and providers of things like financial services to benefit from the growing presence of this population of consumers.

Decline of the Dollar

It is my fervent belief that international investors will, at some time in the coming years, lose faith in the American government's ability to meet its debt obligations. With the aforementioned demographic trends in the United States and the well-known insolvency of the Social Security system, the pressures of increased Medicare spending, and the realities of post-9/11 defense spending, the United States has been led into tremendous deficit spending. I believe that foreign investors and governments are going to consider the entire balance sheet of the United States and come to realize that these growing obligations make it substantially harder for the U.S. government to service its debt. Add to this the fact that the euro has emerged as an alternative currency in which foreign central banks can store their foreign currency reserves, and incremental demand for the U.S. dollar is likely to diminish in the future.

Countries like China and oil-exporting countries that benefit from high oil prices must consider the currency in which they want to store their growing foreign currency reserves. The U.S. dollar has been the default currency for these reserves for many years. This highly liquid instrument, backed by the full faith and credit of the U.S. government, and the largest economy in the world, has been a logical place for other governments to store their excess wealth. When you hear about some $800 billion of foreign currency reserves in China, the vast majority of these are actually being held in U.S. dollars, mostly in the form of investments in U.S. Treasury securities. However, the growing presence of the euro zone as a viable challenge to the status of the United States as the sole economic superpower provides central bankers with an alternative currency to consider using for their savings.

Recent noises by the South Koreans and Chinese that they are moving to a basket of currencies that more appropriately reflects their total trade picture sent shudders through the foreign exchange markets and put pressure on the U.S. dollar. Imagine that a country like China, with its current $800 billion of foreign currency reserves, decides that instead of being 100 percent in U.S. dollars they'll move to perhaps 80 percent U.S. dollars and 20 percent euros. As a stakeholder in the U.S. dollar, the Chinese government doesn't want to dump dollars on the market and buy euros because that would lower the value of their U.S. dollar holdings in a very direct way. Even a large liquid market like that for the U.S. dollar would probably take a hit from the sudden appearance of $160 billion for sale. What China would likely do in such a situation is slow its purchase of dollars and accelerate its purchase of Euros in an attempt to achieve the 80/20 balance. Although this would not be as severe as the impact of a massive sale of dollars, the trend is the same. Incrementally, the Chinese would not be buying dollars but would instead be buying euros. Thus, this very significant buyer of dollars would no longer be a dollar buyer.

At the same time, demand for the euro has increased dramatically. In this situation, the dollar will decline in value relative to the euro and the euro will appreciate relative to the dollar. Now imagine that not just China does this but many countries around the world. Suddenly there would be a lot less demand for dollars and a lot more demand for other currencies.

Combined with the declining creditworthiness of the U.S. government in the eyes of international investors, which I believe will result from the increasing commitments that the U.S. government budget has in terms of health care, pensions, and defense, this structural shift in the foreign exchange markets could lead to a dramatic decline of the dollar. The best way for U.S. investors to protect themselves from this is to take some of their dollars—which, if my thesis is correct, are currently highly valued relative to their future value—and use them to buy foreign assets, which could take the form of property overseas or, much more simply, might follow one of the many international investment ideas outlined in this book. If you use $100 today to buy assets in Russia, France, Japan, or China and in the future your $100 gets you less of the foreign currency, you've done well to protect some of the value of your investment portfolio by making the purchase now. This is a another way of saying that you should have at least 20 percent—and probably 30 percent—of your portfolio in foreign investments if you share any of these concerns about the future position of the dollar. Not only is there the opportunity to benefit from the higher growth and often better prospects in some of these markets, but also you will be able to protect some of your investment portfolio from the decline in value that would result from a decline in the dollar. Although I don't know exactly when this adjustment will take place and I can't say how big it will be, it seems to me that the international trend is toward a less important U.S. dollar and perhaps lower confidence in the U.S. economic situation.

Trade

I am a firm believer that trade will continue to grow in the coming years. Even if the U.S. dollar does decline, there will continue to be strong growth in trade. A cheaper dollar makes U.S. exports cheaper, which would mean more trade out of the United States. While we are waiting for that adjustment to take place, however, the United States will continue to consume considerable amounts of imported goods from China and other places that support trade inbound to the United States. As economies around the world continue to grow and specialize in certain types of business or in parts of the value chain, trade will grow. As a result, investors think-ing about opportunities for the next 3, 5, 10, or 20 years should seriously consider investments related to ship-ping and cargo transport. There are a multitude of ship-building plays, port operators, air freight companies, and logistics companies that could provide a good long-term theme for an investment portfolio.

That is my assessment of investment opportunities looking forward. Visit www.findingthehotspots.com for periodic updates of my views on these and other trends. I believe that changing demographics will have a big impact on economies around the world, that the U.S. dollar will decline in value, and that trade will continue to grow.

Now you know where some of my investments are. I encourage you spend some time thinking about the impact of foreign businesses and growing globalization on your life, your business, and your portfolio. Interna-tional investing is a necessity for the twenty-first century. Not only does it provide diversification and opportunity for profits, but it teaches us about the world and helps protect some of our hard-earned dollars. Best of luck to you in using the tools, strategies, and structures outlined in this book. Happy investing.

Appendix

Throughout this book I have used a one-page data sheet that I developed for my institutional service to provide a quick snapshot of the situation with a given company. The following defines the major terms used on these sheets. Please visit www.findingthehotspots .com for blank copies of this form to fill out on your own for companies that you are considering investing in. This can be a useful way to assemble relevant information in one place.

Dividend: Companies pay dividends as a way of sharing their profits with their shareholders. This is usually presented as the amount of a dividend per share (e.g., cents per share or dollars per share).

52-week range: The highest and lowest price at which the stock has closed over the past year of trading. It

201

is worth noting whether a stock is the highest it has been over the past year or the lowest—though this information on its own will not tell you much about its attractiveness as an investment.

Sector: Sector refers to the industry that the company is in. For example, Microsoft would be in the technology sector, or perhaps it would be considered the software sector. General Motors is considered to be in the automotive sector.

U.S. ticker: The companies discussed in this book have multiple listings in different markets around the world. In most cases they will have a listing in their home market as well as a listing in the United States. This is the stock code that refers to the U.S. listing.

Yield: This is simply the dividend per share divided by the price per share, which gives you the percentage of the purchase price that you will be getting back in the form of a dividend. This also can be considered the interest that you will earn while you are invested in the company. If there is a 5 percent dividend yield on a stock, you might regard it as similar to the interest rate on a savings account (though more risky, as the company could choose to not pay a dividend).

Sales and Earnings

CF/S: Cash flow per share. There are a few different methods to calculate this. I use *gross cash flow*, which is net income plus depreciation, to represent the cash earnings of a company. This is an important number because it represents the amount of cash that a company has to invest in its business and pay down debt.

EBITDA: Earnings before interest, taxes, depreciation, and amortization. This is a useful measure of the earning power of a company. It is especially useful for comparisons of companies across borders, as it avoids the confusion of different depreciation and amortization rules and different tax laws.

EPS: Earnings per share. This is simply the net profit divided by the number of shares outstanding. Sometimes this can be confusing because there are different types of shares that are outstanding.

FY ends: This is the month that the fiscal year ends. Typically, this would be December, but in some countries (such as India) there is a convention of having the fiscal year end in March for most companies.

Net profit: Total bottom-line profit. This is the amount of profit attributable to shareholders.

Pretax profit: Profit before tax.

Sales: Total revenues for the company.

Key Ratios

Average growth rates: This is a useful way to look at longer-term trends in a business. It is especially helpful to note when profits are growing faster or slower than revenues. This can be the first sign that things are going well or poorly for a company.

EBITDA margin: This is calculated as EBITDA divided by total revenues. This is a useful measure of the company's ability to generate earnings.

Pretax margin: This is calculated as pretax income divided by total revenues.

ROE: Return on equity. This is a measure of the company's ability to make profits from the money it has invested. Note that because of the impact of interest expenses on taxable income, ROE can be boosted in companies that have a lot of debt, so if you see a high ROE make sure to check the debt levels.

Sales growth: Percentage growth in revenues or sales.

Valuation

FV/EBITDA: Firm value/EBITDA. This is one of my favorite measures to use, especially when I'm looking at stocks in multiple countries. The firm value is the amount of equity and debt the company has. Calculating this involves taking the market cap (see under "Share Data") and adding any outstanding debt to get the firm value. This allows you to see how much the market (both equity and debt) is valuing the company. You then divide this by the EBITDA.

P/CFLO per share: Price/cash flow per share. Calculated using the cash flow (discussed above) and the number of shares and is a slightly more useful measure of the valuation of a stock. It does a better job than P/E but is less widely used, as people calculate it in many different ways.

P/E: Price-earnings ratio. This is calculated as price per share divided by earnings per share. This is the most universally discussed measure of valuation of a stock. Though flawed because of differences in cash flow measurements, it is useful because it is so widely used and followed.

Price/book: Often referred to as P/B, this is calculated as the price per share divided by the value of the assets on the balance sheet per share. Think of this in your own context. If you added up the value of your bank deposits, your house, and your car, that sum would represent your total assets, or your book value.

Price/revs: Price/revenues multiple. This is calculated as the price per share divided by the revenues per share. It is not very useful except in situations where a company is not making profits and you need to have some way to measure how the price relates to the operations of the company.

Balance Sheet Summary

Current assets: These are assets that a company can get its hands on quickly. Consider inventories, cash, checking accounts, easily salable stocks and bonds, and similar items to be current assets.

Current liabilities: These are things that you owe which are going to be due in the next year. Consider this the portion of your mortgage that you have to pay this year.

Equity: This is often referred to as *shareholder's equity*. This is the value that the shareholders have built up in the business. This is the value of the business and its assets above and beyond any debts that are outstanding.

Fixed assets: This includes longer-term assets such as buildings, improvements to factories, and things that you probably could not sell off quickly if you needed to.

Long-term debt: This includes the things that you have to pay back over a period of time, longer than a year.

L-T debt/capital: Long-term debt/total capital. This is a measure of how much debt a company has outstanding.

Other assets: This often includes what are called *intangible assets*, such as the value of a brand name or trademark, or some reflection of the value of contracts that you have.

Share Data

Avg. daily vol. (000): Average daily volume in thousands of shares. This is the number of shares that have traded, on average, per day (we use the average from the past 90 days).

Avg. daily vol. (U.S.$): This is the average daily volume presented in terms of U.S. dollars.

Float: The number of shares that are actually free to trade. Often if a company has a large government ownership or ownership from another company this reduces the float.

Insider ownership: The percentage of shares owned by insiders (management or people who have some connection to the company).

Institutional ownership: The percentage of shares owned by institutional investors, including mutual funds and so on.

Market cap (U.S.$ mil.): This is the current share price multiplied by the number of shares outstanding, a useful measure of how much the equity market is willing to pay for a company.

Primary shares: This is the number of shares outstanding.

Index